# THE MAN HAS WINGS

Books by Terence L. Connolly, S.J., Ph.D.

*The Poems of Francis Thompson*
edited with notes

*Francis Thompson: In His Paths*

Coventry Patmore's
*Mystical Poems of Nuptial Love*
edited with notes

*On the Love of God*
a translation into English of
St. Bernard's Latin Treatise

*Literary Criticisms*
*By Francis Thompson*
newly discovered and collected

# *The Man Has Wings*

NEW POEMS AND PLAYS

*by*

*Francis Thompson*

AUTHOR OF "THE HOUND OF HEAVEN"

Edited with Preface & Notes
by TERENCE L. CONNOLLY, S.J., Ph.D.

DIRECTOR OF LIBRARIES AND CURATOR
OF THE THOMPSON COLLECTION
BOSTON COLLEGE

HANOVER HOUSE, GARDEN CITY, NEW YORK

*Library of Congress Catalog Card Number 57-11414*




*Printed in the United States of America*

FIRST EDITION

TO

MY BROTHER JIM

IN

LOVING AND DEVOTED MEMORY

# PREFACE

It is a wise poet who tempers his flight to his wings' strength as Thompson does in the poems here collected. In them there is no straining to reach the empyrean that gave us the highest achievement of *Poems* and *New Poems*. And yet, Thompson soars somewhat between earth and heaven in these poems. Many of them compare favorably with the lesser poems in his published works, and none of them, it is hoped—recognized, as they may be, of secondary importance—will detract from his established reputation as a poet. The reader who reads for pure enjoyment cannot fail to find a measure of delight in these pages, and those who read for amusement, only, will catch a glimpse, too seldom vouchsafed, of the poet at play, as he shakes his cap and bells in the section of light verse. Only a pedant would judge that Chesterton's nonsense verses and Belloc's *Cautionary Tales* detract from their reputations as poets. And there would seem to be little reason for regarding Thompson less a poet because of his light verse with its delightful sense of humor that must, happily, modify his too general reputation as a poet of unrelieved grimness. These verses are the poet's answer to his own questioning in *The Poet Jester:*

> Must one *always* work nought else
> Than the high phantastic spells?

The poems and plays in the following pages—with the exception of *The Schoolmaster for God*—are here printed for the first time. They have been selected from manuscripts in the Francis Thompson Collection at Boston College which includes more than a hundred notebooks and nearly eight hundred manuscripts of poetry and prose, to which have been recently added the original manuscripts of *The Hound of Heaven* and the "Essay on Shelley."

In attempting an arrangement of material so diverse in theme and treatment, an effort has been made to respect Thompson's preference for "a chronological arrangement or some form of classification." When there is no title in a manuscript, one is supplied and enclosed in brackets, and brackets are also used to enclose a word that is doubtful because indistinct. From rough drafts and corrected copy, the version selected appears to be the one of

Thompson's preference. Brief notes at the end of the volume indicate the location of manuscripts and, in a few instances, explain topical allusions.

Of the two plays, *Napoleon Judges* is not without merit, literary and dramatic. But it is too brief for presentation unless as an *intermède* on a program of one-act plays. In the hope that it might be considered for publication, Thompson once sent it to William Archer, by whom it was rejected, as it was later when submitted to *T. P.'s Weekly*. In *Man Proposes, But Woman Disposes* there is little dramatic action and much talk—"full of ready-made jibes and laboriously smart give-and-take," in Everard Meynell's opinion. Thompson must have been aware of the dramatic weakness of the piece, when he added beneath the title: *Un conte sans raconteur*.

In the Patmore Collection at Boston College is a letter (August 31, 1897) from Coventry Patmore's son, Tennyson, to Forbes Robertson, suggesting a meeting with Thompson who was anxious to show the actor "a tiny drama" [probably *Napoleon Judges*], to discuss "its suitability for the stage." The letter was never delivered and subsequent efforts to have Thompson meet those experienced in dramatic production proved futile, chiefly because of the poet's dilatoriness and excessive shyness.

T. L. C.

## ACKNOWLEDGMENTS

For tireless research among manuscripts of the Boston College Collection of Thompsoniana, the editor is hopelessly indebted to MISS MARTHA DUBAY of the Boston College Library staff. The typing and arrangement of material for publication, the work of MRS. RICHARD E. LISHERNESS, has been an indispensable help. To her and to members of the Library Staff for their patient response to numberless demands, the editor wishes to express his sincerest thanks. The encouragement and help of MR. JOHN J. DELANEY of Hanover House in his sympathetic reading and editing of the manuscript is acknowledged with deepest gratitude.

# CONTENTS

# *POEMS*

# A POETIC SEQUENCE

## I. ELIJAH

When the old prophet's spirit murmurèd
For famine, loneliness, necessitude,
God sent the bird far-visitant which fed
His bitter need, and his sick heart renewed.
No less to me, with spirit all o'ertasked,
God hath sent gentlest succour, and a boon
My rashest tongue as hopefully had asked
As hang petitions on the horns o' the moon.
Whence I resume my fortitude, and hold
The perilous verges of the appointed way,
Even to that spot predestined and foretold
Where, on a nigh-at-hand implacable day,
(Long shown and known in what
prenuntiant gloom!)
The sudden gulf goes down to dreadful doom.

## II. WAITING

Behold, behold!
Come hither; thaw from out their torpid cold
My thoughts, as weeds in waters are
Congealed with severe frost; how far,
Through the cold mind's unmoving mere,
In rigid mockery they appear
Of the life which they have not!
It is not that thou art forgot;
But thou, a most remembered day
Of summer when shrewd skies are grey,
Giv'st to the too palpable chill

Contrast, not comfort, howsoe'er I will.
Ah, break my leaden broodings through
With a ray of very you!
A dream of you has wrought me wrong,
Wherein one smile was all your tongue;
I woke—alas, my heart frost-stricken
Only into live ache did quicken!
Like an odour whose fine fume
One weak moment doth relume
The ruined sun of fallen fields:
The vision parts in tears, and yields
Pang to the poor heart and brain
For a dead day dead again.

Ah, is it dead indeed! I cry;
Ah, is it dead, which still can die?
Or is your friendship live? then give
Its life to me, that I may live!
I trust; O help thou my untrust!
The soul stands fast, yet the heart must,
In soul's despite, with this thought sicken—
O is that quick, which doth not quicken?

## III. FORGOING

The white wings come no more: out through the gloom
I look,—no, no, no more! My prayer not fell
Unanswered; she hath made a speedy doom.
Well, it was well; you have done all things well.
I do believe some tender wisdom bade
Your choice; I unreproaching, friend late dear,
Say, *Fiat.* I am sad, that now was glad;
The last smile is o'ertaken in a tear,
Ere it had time to die, making fair weeping.
A butterfly, that brushes some dark thing,
Some dusty splendour leaves unto its keeping;
And some good thoughts, late fallen from your wing,
Tell what bright visitant one moment lit
On my sad spirit, and then fled from it.

## IV. ["SO NOW, GIVE O'ER"]

So now, give o'er; for you are lost, I see,
And this poor babe was dead even its birth,
Which I had thought a young Joy born to me,
Who had no child but Sorrow: and with mirth
I gazed upon its face, nor knew it dead,
And in my madness vowed that it did smile;
I said: "Dear Soul, learn laughter, leave thy shed
Sore tears, put off thy mourning weeds a while.
This is our child a space, even though it die
Hereafter; laugh a season, though it be
Thy tears are but sad jewels thou put'st by,
One day to wear again." Very wan she
Tried, doubting, unused smiles; then bowed her head:—
"Much tears have made thee blind: this, too, is dead!"

# LOVE VERSES

## ["THIS VESSEL MAN"]

This vessel man, unloaden of rich love,
Lists, and no longer floats with even keel.
Such costly lading was designed by Jove
To keep her firm, who lacking it must heel.
Stern is the captain-spirit that yet can sail
His hull untreasured safe into the gale.

## [THE SOLEMN VOICE]

Do I not hear the solemn voice,
The voice which I have heard so long,
Which says: "Stand like a lonely tower
Amidst the grim lean life which works thee wrong.
Thrust down thy heart: teach Love himself
To dread the shaking of the whip,
And fold his lovely passionate wings,
Nor moan against the deadly hurt of things!"
I hear the wind drum and the long rain drip;
I keep the lonely-burning thought of thee
Trimmed in my lonely heart,
And all apart
It flickers in the passionate wind
Of longing; with a stern-set mind
I work and watch it patiently.
I have endured, and I endure;
I know it is the bitter blast
Of sacrifice which sifts the pure
Snow of the love which lofty souls'
Pained peaks enstoles;
I have stood fast, and I stand fast.
But O, rebuke me not if sometimes at the last

Love wakens with a shrill and piercing cry
Amid my life's wide arid sand,
Crying with power
No menace of the will can stay:
"O for one hour
To look again into her very eye!
O, for one vital day,
Feel the lost Eden of her very hand!"
O friend! that rebel cry dies down;
And I am king still in my iron crown.

## [FALSE LOVE AND TRUE]

You have had women at your beck,
And women at your call;
Many have hung around your neck
Their girdle virginal.

You have lain amid a lair of curls,—
And yet, when all is done,
Though you have loved a dozen girls,
You never have loved one!

O you have loved in many ways,
Dainty, and fierce, and light;
And some were sweet, and all were base,
And now you hold love slight.

You who have loved in many climes,
And under many suns:
You who have loved so many times,
You never have loved once!

You have loved dark, you have loved fair,
The black eye and the blue,
The swart, the brown, the red-gold hair,
Loved all complexions through.

Ah fool! he misses still, who roves,
The thing for which all rove:
You who have known so many loves,
You never have known love!

## ["HER FEET ARE EARTH"]

Her feet are earth, and her face is heaven,
Her breast is the young moon's half-grown round;
The stars move over her eyes of Even,
And night impends in her hair half-bound.
What if no body she have for embracing?
What if no heart she have to prize him?
She can do what a maiden can:—
Yield her face to her poet's praising,
Yield her eyes to her lover's gazing,
With a more gracious favour despise him,
Than maidens use when they love a man.

## ["I LOVE AND HATE THEE"]

I love and hate thee, seeing that my love
Tears thee from Him that loves thee, from the Love
Which made thee for His Love, and casts thee down
The abysmal love that counterchanges name
With Hate and Death, but in its counterchange
Keeps one unchanging essence.

## ["YOU, WHILE THE GALE YOUR LOCKS UNBINDS"]

You, while the gale your locks unbinds,
Exult to hear the talking shrouds:
I fear a meaning in the winds,
And ask an oracle of the clouds.

Ah, for my sake, have thou more heed,
Not to brave thee, but fearful me:
And bring me back secure, I plead,
From thy imagined jeopardy!

If thy soul, gaily fugitive,
To join its kindred plumes were freed:—
Why thou, dear dead, wouldst then most live;
While I, who lived, were dead indeed!

## ["AS MORNING EYES FROM SLEEP AWAKENING"]

As morning eyes from sleep awakening
Upon a shining casement, briefly glimpsed,
Close back to darkness, but the dazzled gloom
Still keeps the inward vision; so my heart
Asleep to love, did open upon thee,
And took on the sudden vision of thy face,
And from the brief irradiant four years' glimpse
Closing again to darkness of all love,
Sees nothing but that face.

## ["WAKE NOT THE STILL SAD YEARS"]

Wake not the still sad years,
Thou canst not cure, if they should wake too sore.
O sweet! no sweetness withers in my heart,
For none was to impart
What only comes from others' fragrancing.
Of pleasantness I have not any art,
In this grief-erudite heart!
O sweet! I pray thee, spare thy pitying;
Because my many wounds, late ichored o'er,
Melt and are gallèd by thy dropping tears.
O sweet! thou canst not love; not in thy power
The extreme sweet for my exceeding sour.

## *VALETE*

We have been comrades, and I dwelled with you;
You have been sportful, and I played with you;
You have been mirthful, and I laughed with you;
You have been tearful, and I kissed with you;
You have been selfful, and I bare with you;
You have been loveful, and I loved with you;
You have been strifeful, and I strove with you:
Now it is ended, and I part with you.
You have been happy, you and I with you,
And many happy flowers bear home with you;
I my one flower, and my one flower is dead.

## TO CECILIA

Musing on that Cecily,
Music's Saint, and Saint of thee,
I thought how once her lover spied
An angel by her lilied side.
To myself then said I: "Ah!
By mine own sweet Cecilia
Whence is it I see not one
Skiey winged companion;
Though angels might, on her to wait,
Jostle in heaven's hindering gate?"
I, for answer mute a space,
Looked, and found it in her face.—
Not an angel of them all,
Luminous, majestical,
Mated with this maiden tall,
Not an angel of them all
Would for a right angel pass,
Beside the angel that she was.

## *NISI DOMINUS*

*Nisi Dominus ædificaverit domum, in vanum laboraverunt qui ædificant eam.* (Ps. CXXVI, I.)

Alack! how have the gates of hell prevailed
Against this spirit, and its firm mortise failed
This spirit of mine, which thou and I have raised
On secret heights where but God's eagles gazed!
In vain we pile with our poor human hands
Stone upon stone, until the building stands
Irradiate in completed purity,
Unless the Holy One its keystone be.
Except the Lord have builded and have knit
This house of aspirant spirit, is it not writ
In vain we labour who have builded it?
Like to the tower on Sennaar rose sublime,
It rests a nayword to successive time.
Confusion of tongues is come on us, God wot!
And that which I would speak, thou understandest not.

## ["THE PERFECT WOMAN"]

(To follow *"Domus Tua"*)

The perfect woman? who may she,
I prythee, be?
The perfect woman see in her,
Alone, who is a Christ-bearer.
Yet in fair form of every woman,
However frailly all too human,
Divine pavilion do I see,
Although, perchance, defeatedly.
A tenement for God and Peace,
Though Strife and Satan have the lease.

## TO A WIND

Breeze that meetest *her* mouth,
  Wing unto me here!
I should know the breath you bare
  From all breath less dear.

I should know your soft fall
  From all gales less dear;
I should say: "My friend's breath
  Sighs in my ear."

Oh, from every meaner breeze
  Blowing West or South,
I should know the breeze had blown
  Across her fragrant mouth!

## THE BRIDE OF GOD AND THEE

Of loftiest worship would'st thou know
  The test? 'tis when thou canst espy
This truth:—thy lady is more low
  Than thou, and therefore is more high;
When thy right potence of command
  Thou canst retain with reverence sweet;
And the proud secret understand,
  To sway her, duteous at her feet.
In term and lowlihead Man is crowned;
  And she, the bride of God and thee,
Is doubly Bride, and doubly Bound,
  And so the Man peculiarly.
Because the ruler from the ruled
  Takes rule, thou shalt take rule from her,
And yet shalt rule her; nor be schooled
  By what the blind and fools aver.
Save Man be not God's subject, this
  Is fixed as are the roots of heaven:
Yet she's thine equal; for there is

By place no right equality riven.
Or thus I paradox the thing,
And let the wise take what I mean;—
That thou shalt rule her as her King,
And she shall rule thee as thy Queen.
Thou art the first, the second she;
Yet in thine homage be this reversed,
Knowing God doth delightedly
With him the Last ordain the First.
These things I utter; but who doth them is
The woman's servant, for the woman's his.

## *DE MORTUIS*

Yester-hour, Sweet, you were a child
(To me, at least, so old and sad),
Sweet-briar buds out of April's font
Recent, hailed "Sister!" and were glad.

To-day, the height, whence Noah saw
A drowned world's face up-float amid
The waters, is less old; or years
Sanded about the Pyramid;

You are more old than agèd brine
Which scurfed the dragon-pressed seaweed;
Yet young, past antenatal bloom
That biggens the unseeded seed.

Girl, you can lesson the white beard to-day!
And sedulous Science shall expound—
A thousand peering years to be—
What your fair eyes have early found.

With greater and with lesser tube
Are careful generations pained
To search the bones o' the world.—Sweet child,
You beat your wing, and you attained!

Yesterday's simple kneeler, now
  Who smilest holier philosophy
Than schools disputing!—Who didst list
  My song, the stars now hush for thee;

So quick the inward music breaks
  When rended is the dyke of flesh;
So swift the fledged escaping songs
  Mount from the broken body's mesh.

To us the crumbs of song and knowledge; you
  Have the high table, and are calm.
We munch with earth-bowed head, nor look
  Where your full feast is wreathed with palm.

Ah, wherefore do we dim-eyed race of men
    For knowledge root, and vaunt of that we know,
Since Death so great a master is,
  And of his teaching is not slow?

When you, child, to out-learn us all,
  Did but from our dull converse rise,
And, bedward somewhat early ere the dark,
  Let out the light, Sweet, and your eyes.

## FRAGMENT OF HELL

My friends, ye weep around my bed,—for me—
Weep not! pray, pray! put one life in a prayer
To hold me back, for I am going, dying—
Oh pray! pray all! one prayer!—what can tears do?
For I sink, sink, clutch earth as in a nightmare,
Slipping by inches—one prayer, one,—for me,
Will you not pray for me, for your own me,
Your son, your cousin, brother, friend,
Who die, who drop into eternal fires,
And cannot pray,—prayer?—I ne'er prayed myself!
Oh! soul's hope! pray!—Weep, weep?—can tears quench
  hell?

## AN UNAMIABLE CHILD

"A child unsweet of face or air,
Childhood's sworn amorists put her by;
Nothing to love I see in her."
Nothing. A sad God's-truth. Nor I.
Because there is nothing to love her for,
Good need is it that I love her the more;
Because she's unlovesome, I needs must love
With all the love that she cannot move;
For that *you* cannot love her, you
Have left your love for me to do.
Nothing to love in her I see,
Except it be the very she.
They who love what all men crave,
Fearing to lose, scarce seem to have;
But never fear can overcome me
Lest men steal this sweet nothing from me:
Nothing to love I sweetly choose,
So, sweetly safe nothing to lose.
Because you have nothing that world's love
charms,
I clasp you, child, with the whole world's arms.
Yet—yet—ah, if it should befall,
To have nothing, and lose it all!

## ["GO, BOOK, THOU SHALT BE HAPPIER"]

Go, book, thou shalt be happier
Than I; thou shalt approach to her
Who is sealed up from me like Paradise,
Shalt fall into her blissful power,
And be the happy captive of her hand.
Long since I fell into her power;
O for one hour
To be again
In that white tyranny of her reign,

With sweet surprise
Fall in the ambush of her sudden eyes,
And for one moment stand
The happy, happy captive of her hand!
But I am banished into freedom; thou
Shalt never break thy bands,
Nor fate compel
Wretched deliverance from her heavenly hands;
But in that —— clime for ever dwell
Of her Hesperian eyes,
That country of her presence, where do blossom
Flowing with milk and honey of her bosom,
Wherein all goods and mercies have their rise.

Tell her, my book,
Tell her she need not look
For happy thoughts in thee,
Fitting her company;
Tell her I send
Too sad a messenger
For my glad friend;
For how from me should any comfort come,
Expatriated from my home
Of native her?

And ah, my book, retain some air
Of me,
Thy master, that when she
O'er thee shall bend,
A little touch a little while
May her beguile,
Half-conscious, of her friend,
Hopeless and faithful to the patient end.

# SONNETS

## *ECCE ANCILLA DOMINI*

(*National Gallery*)

This angel's feet, winged with aspiring light,
  That kindles its own image in the floor;
His gravely noble face, serene in might
  From gazing on the Godhead evermore;
This lily shining from the lilied land,
  Making a breath of heaven in the room;
Yon dove, whose presence tells how near at hand
  The mystical conception of her womb:
Were *these* the things that roused from holy dreams
  To holier waking the elected maid?
Absorbed in all the great to-be she seems,
  With pensive eyes that yet are not afraid.
    Soon her low voice shall ratify heaven's will,
    And hell's gate groan, and death's stern heart stand
      still.

## ["A BITTER FRIEND"]

A bitter friend, sweet Friend, you have of me!
  How rash of speech, and how unfixed of mood!
Like to the gray-green Holly of the Sea,
  Its very flower to tender touches rude.
A fruit unlovely, and most harsh of rind,
  Is that best homage which I do profess;
And my best kind so twisted with unkind
  As wounds your hand with proffered tenderness.
For so sweet friend a bitter friend! Let be:
  I am no comrade for your gentle years;
Save were I quite repured, and all of me

Recrystallizèd from dissolvent tears.
Save this could be, O better thou shouldst part
From me, dear Friend, who canst not from my heart!

## ["ALACK! MY DEEP OFFENCE"]

Alack! my deep offence is kneaded in
Even with the very stuff of poetry;
So that, sore striving with the ungracious sin,
Defeat comes hard on my best victory.
Even as a victor, feasting in his tent,
That is surprisèd by the beaten foe,
Losing the purchase of his hardiment,
From the overthrown receives his overthrow.
Enough for me the sick unfruit of toil,
And the won fight to be won o'er again;
But ah, the pang! when that within-turmoil
Means to thee pain, my dear, and to thee pain!
For the renewed fight I am sad and strong;
But stand from me, lest it should do *thee* wrong!

## ["WHAT HAVE I LEFT"]

What have I left, fair friend, to say to thee,
That to another gave a topless praise?
Wilt thou not chide: "Have done, your songs of me
Are dulled and scandalled by those former lays"?
My verse had never lie in mouth: I do
Unpraise no jot that I did praise of her;
What I have writ is writ—one comment true,
That these things were, I would it were not "were"!
Deserved she so? The dearer must I rate
Thee, then, that to her most canst be a more,

Out-marvelling marvel: though thine estimate,
Friend, I can match not from my bankrupt store
Who Song's mere prodigal before thee stand,
His gold all spent and no price in his hand.

## [MY SONG'S YOUNG VIRGIN DATE]

Yea, she that had my song's young virgin date,
Not now, alas, that noble singular she,
I nobler hold, though marred from her once state,
Than others in their best integrity.
My own stern hand has rent the ancient bond,
And thereof shall the ending not have end:
But not for me, that loved her, to be fond
Lightly to please me with a newer friend.
Then hold it more than bravest-feathered song,
That I affirm to thee, with heart of pride,
I knew not what did to a friend belong
Till I stood up, true friend, by thy true side;
Whose absence dearer comfort is, by far,
Than presences of other women are!

## ADVERSITY

My soul in desolate royalty of woe
Sits diademed with sorrow as a crown,
All misery's blazing jewelry aglow
On melancholy's dim, majestic gown.
She, wont to sport unblamed with Poetry,
Music and Painting, boundlessly content,
Accepted playmate of the glorious three,
For only viol now has loud lament!
And Poetry sits weeping through her hair,
And Painting's eye is misty with its tears.

Yet am I to the dead years' riches heir;
Not wholly poor, nor bondslave to my fears.
My spirit feeds, although my body fast,
Amid the garnered memories of the Past.

## [SAD SEMELE]

Who clasp lost spirits, also clasp their hell;
You have clasped, and burn, sad child, sad Semele!
One half of my cup have you drunk too well,
And that's the death; the immortality
Girt in the fiery spirit flies your lip.
That to my deathless progeny of pain
You should be mother, bear your fellowship
I' the mortal grief, without the immortal gain!
Not only I, that these poor verses live,
A heavy vigil keep of parchèd nights;
But you for unborn men your pangs must give,
And wake in tears, that they may dream delights.
What poems be, Sweet, you did never know;
And yet are poems suckled by your woe!

## ["LOVE, THOU HAST SUFFERED"]

Love, thou hast suffered many wrongs of mine,
When my sad youth, for hunger and lack of thee,
Fouled, O most foul, its heavenly plumage fine,
Living on carrion. Yet one wrong from me
Thou hast not had—I have not held thee light.
Once did I love, and was my love betrayed,
So better than betraying: true, with might
I loved, and in the furrow that love made
Perished the seed scarce quickened; yet was this,
And all the sorrow of this, a better thing
Than the sacrilegion of a dallying kiss,

Using thy sanctuary for pleasancing.
  Now all is dark: but yet an august gloom,
  Being gravely equalled with a solemn doom.

## *UNE FILLE DE JOIE*

Hell's gates revolve upon her yet alive;
  To her no Christ the beautiful is nigh:
  The stony world has daffed his teaching by;
"Go!" saith it; "Sin on still that you may thrive,
Let one sin be as queen for all the hive
  Of sins to swarm around; while I, chaste I,
  In cheap immaculateness avert mine eye:—
Poor galley-slave of lust, rot in your gyve!"
This is her doom! The ways are barriered which
  Should lead to the All-Merciful's abode;
  The house of penitence which Mary trod
Long since is grown an appanage of the rich:
    And though she strive, yea, strive and strive, *how* strive!—
    The gates of Hell have shut her in alive.

# A CHORIC SONG

## CHORIC SONG OF FAUNS

Each a little furnace-glow
Darting go
Bees unquenchable, and blow
Each his furry clarinet.
Owl, screech!
Croak, frog!
Whine to me,
Hedgehog!
I do know your every speech,
Master bee
I can teach
How to hum his alphabet!

Lo, the bats that to and fro
Drifting go,
Like blown flakes of dusky snow
That presage the storm of night.
Piece of night! take your flight,
Flitter-mouse!
Do not fright
Me who house
Like a squirrel in the boughs.

Hark the hyacinth! it chatters
Fragrant matters,
And its pretty prattle scatters,
Clung in cluster sapphirine.
Earth and sun to frame it twine;
Yea, and this
Odour fine
Nothing is
But the breath o' their meeting kiss.

When the winter-trees are strowing
Nuts for sowing,
And my winter-coat is growing,
An acorn-feast is a mess for the gods!
When my hoof i' the crunched snow plods,
Nostrils steam
As we snort,
Grinding the frozen stream
In sport;
By Pan's truth,
Then the berry is sweet in tooth!

Sweet is nymph in shade,
With lilies loitering in her lapsèd hair:
Sweet no less
When the sliding measures of her tress
The sere ambers and cornelians braid
Of leaves that slip
O'er her deep eyes, and drip
Adown her moonbeam shoulder bare:
Most sweet is maid
With autumn lingering in her loosèd hair.
Sweet are all times to them that can
With Sylvan dwell and Pan,
And every season fair.

Yet now come hither,
Before the May moon wither,
While the daffodilly
Is fresh remembered by the inconstant year;
Ere slip beneath the mere
With her womb's burthen the espousèd lily;
Or ere the sun's averted looks turn cold,
And the earth sighs, and knows that she is old!

# A MISCELLANY

## ["'BEAUTY IS TRUTH, TRUTH BEAUTY'"]

"Beauty is truth, truth beauty," well thou saidst,
Boy of the ages!
For to itself the toad seems beautiful,
And beauty's self is in dull censure dull.

## ["ALL THINGS ARE JOY"]

All things are joy, all things are light,
The spider's feet a-labouring
From silken tulips exquisite
Its lacy round of argent sling.

The tremulous dragonfly in wonder
Regards his eyes' twin gleaming spheres
Within the splendent pool, whereunder
Spawns a mysterious universe.

'Neath the woods, where but hushed noises cross,
The shy fawn keeps a-dream its games;
In the green casket of the moss
The live gold of the scarab flames.

## ["I SAT WITH NATURE"]

I sat with Nature in a wood
Full of silence that was sound,
And of throngèd solitude;
And I bound
All my pulses to attend her,
Were she in the babbling-mood.

I and Nature sat apart.
She might teach me if she would
The silence at the silence' heart,
The solitude
That makes the solitude. Her gazes
Did not know that she was sued.

I sat with Nature's loveliness,
Unapparelled for me,
And her eyes of wistfulness
I could see
Meant me not. The murmured meanings
Of her mouth were God's, I guess.

## GENESIS

A little brown seed, on the breezes blown,
Fell to earth in a land unknown;
Whither it drifted it knew not, nor
What was the secret its bosom bore.

No fairness was its to take men's heed,
Of the little brown stranger they knew no need:
Itself to itself seemed a futile birth,
And it sank or was trampled into the earth.

As it lay in earth, as it lay in earth,
Itself to itself but a futile birth,
With the worm and the insect for company,
Its soul grew sterile, its heart turned dry.

Frost barred the doors of its prisoning mould,
Where it lay in hunger, and dark, and cold,
And after the frost came the drenching rain,
Till dulled and lethargied, pained out of pain,

It recked no longer of rains that beat,
Nor the pitiless chill, nor the trampling feet;
And when hastening Spring sent her voice before,
It lay in swoon, with a palsied core.

At length did a tender sunshine come
With fostering warmth to it, shrivelled and numb,
And the seed awoke in the earth apart
To stirrings wild, and a pang at the heart.

The new life stabbed it with jaggèd pains,
As when blood is rash-thawed in curdled veins;
And, like lightning crouched panting within the storm,
Its bosom was heaved by some vital form.

It struggled, foreseeing not, blindly pained,
To what were its throes and itself ordained;
Till at last to the very heart it split,—
And only a little shoot burst from it.

But the little shoot grew to a lusty shoot,
While the cloven seed fell from the deepening root;
While the lusty shoot opened a radiant bloom,
The seed rotted into an earthy tomb.

Fragrance blew wide from the beautiful flower,
And maidens bore it into their bower,
But under their tread, its mission done,
The dissolved seed felt not the rain or sun.

So it must be; the seed must throe,
And its heart be rent, that the flower may grow,
Be rent to the heart for the beautiful flower
That maidens cherish within their bower.

So it must be, while Fate has power,
To earth the seed, the blossom to bower:
The flower was meet for a maiden's mouth,
The seed brown, withered with wintry drouth.

The seed was fit but to grow the flower;
And the maid who bends lips to the blossom in bower
Sighs no sigh for the seed, I wis,
That never a maiden had lips to kiss.

## ["SING, BIRD, SING"]

Sing, bird!
Sing, sing thy love with me,
  Sing with no one near us;
Sing, sing thy love with me,
  Till the buds burst forth to hear us!
Mad thy heart with melody,
Sing, sing, and clap thy wing,
  Till thou set thy bough a-swinging.
God, pausing on His ways,
To His angels turns and says:
  "Methinks it is sweet singing!"

Bird, bird! what the thing
Thou dost sing with throbbing wing,
  Twining and adorning
A lay to laugh my low renown,
With the lovely notes that run
From thy throat of beating brown,
When the dancing foot o' the Sun
Shakes the showering blossoms down
  From the bowery morning?

Bird of joy! what the thing
Thou dost sing;
  What thoughts dost thou harbour
When the Sun whom dawn embowers
Dances down the blossomy showers
  From the shaken morning's arbour?
The hovering earth like a bee doth sing
  In the golden shine;
Thy throat is washed with the morning's wine;
Dost thou [hymn] to the Throne divine
  A lonely thing?

"The sun has made his nest,
  Built in the boughs of the night;
The sun has lined his nest in the West
  With soft clouds white.
I sing to my mate in the nest:—
  'O down o' the breast!'
To my love in the nest my song flies:—
  'O rain-drop eyes!'"

The dawning star that fetched her breath
  At the foot-fall of the sun,
She has hidden her head in his outstretched
    arms,
  Goldenly undone.
Ah, wastrel of thy lays!
  Is it but for his coming's mirth
That he kisses the tears from the face
  Of the all-night widowed earth?

For God is praised by this lovely thing,
  And very meet,
As He in Nature's raimenting
Goes forth, about His holy feet
Tinkles our sweet love-singing.
Yea, loves are as the apples of gold
On Aaron's priestly robes of old,
And pure love-songs the bells that hung
Between, and all in a sweet clash swung,
  Godlily ringing.

Hither, descend to me!
  Brothers are we both:
Sit upon thy home-tree,
  Sing, sing thy love-troth.
Surely otherwhere
  Thy morning walks are trod,
Yea, thy winding stair
  Leads to God.

## ["LEARN OF THE MOUTH OF THE MOON"]

Learn of the mouth of the moon,
  If thou wouldst sing of delight;
The night still thinks of the noon,
  When its lady walks in her white.
The night still thinks of the noon,
In the film of her silvern way,
But the song on the lips of the day
  Has an inward tone of the night.

## [PROPHETIC VERSE]

The moon, an apparition ere the night,
With bloody portent of the coming wrath,
Untimely on the ruined day intrudes;
The clinkered sun has gone out sullenly.

The waning moon is tinged with fantasy;
In vain the augurs mark the boding light,
And the dark rack that heaps against her path,
Her beam disastrous o'er the region broods,
And croaking on their way the ravens flee.

Feared nations shrink, and from the omen cower,
The paling prophets speak with lips of doom,
All hatreds in common horror thronged agree;
The stars with veilèd countenance own the power,
The bride's kiss falters from her new-wed groom,
And the sick earth is 'ware of destiny.

## *"MARIA INTRA LIMINA ÆSTUANT"*

Not what wouldst be, in thy blind heart,
But what God willeth thee, thou art.
Learn, darkly with the fates at strife,
To shape thyself within thy life:
In the traced furrow sow thy crops;
Give homage to the checks and stops
Which point thy life's set period,
And circumstance, the goad of God.
Believe, with spirit nigh to break,
Believe for the believing's sake;
When the thwart time its worst has done,
There is some fruit beneath the sun;
Some fruit there is beneath the sun.

## [A FAITHLESS SWORD]

Ah God, a faithless sword, I broke
In Thy right hand, for Thy great stroke
Too weak; or rather, all a-rust,
In such a falchion was no trust,
Which Thou, half-drawn, didst backward thrust
Into the slothful sheath, where laid
Roughed red with sin, the [recreant] blade
Having Thy great intent betrayed,
Foully content; and did not know,
Tried, and unready, strikes no blow.
And now, my Master and my Lord,
Thou castest Thy false-proven sword
Out of Thy hand—is it not so?
And yet, my Master and my Lord,
And yet Thy hand shall lack no sword
Stretched forth against the hissing foe.

Lo!
All things Thou dost aright; and me
Unfaithful though Thou put'st from Thee,
I yet through the hot throat of hell
Shall cry exulting, "It is well!"
Though Thou put by Thy recreant sword,
Yet Thou triumph'st, and Thou art Lord!

## ["HE CAME TO ME"]

He came to me, disguised like daily men;
Nor was there any sign to note him one
Should intercept the stars and sun;
So still were my unprescient pulses then.

Until I woke to find his sudden stature
Come utterly between me and my heaven,
My earth, my dreams, my angels even:
Closer than breath, more everywhere than all my Nature.

Ah! then I marvelled I could think him small
Who stands betrayed insuperably great;
And how my pulses kept their ignorant state,
That haste to serve and tremble at his call!

## [MADONNA AND CHILD]

Bound in a little woman's arms,
Without a language plain;
His feet were on the turning globe,
He held the stars in rein.

His feet were on the turning globe,
The stars His fingers twirled;
His cry was all for mother's milk,
Her lap was all His world.

So in a point was hemmed the Whole,
  The Word was without word;
The Godhead wailed for mother's milk,
  And unafraid she heard.

He asked not spheral lullabies,
  Nor stretched for fanning wings;
Being God, He took with grateful mouth
  Mild, elemental things.

The maiden pearls of virgin milk
  Were food for Him Who fed
Out of His hand the fledgèd worlds—
  She bare up the Godhead.

The Trinity nested in her lap;
  The angels' plumy laughter
At things too sweet for any awe
  Left their lips tender after.

## [WEEP FOR HIM]

O thou, who say'st, "At length men's hapless crew
Know all their haplessness, and know it through;"
Hast, in the little round thy thoughts have trod,
Dreamed on the haplessness of this sweet God?
Man took, in malice, to his tainted vein,
Sin, and its legacy of lazarous pain.
    And the heroic God
    Stooped from His safe abode
  To kiss the infected flesh, and take
The dreadful tetter for His loves' dear sake,
To suck the venom from the ulcerous place,
That man might grope a way to grace,
And on his sick-bed, earth, might fever through his
      pain.

Only for man, ingrate,
That opened merciful gate
To fling to in the mocked God's face again;
Saying—"Thy unasked pardon we reject,
And steadfastly elect
Eternal penalty,
So but we may be free
To hate Thy love, and loathe Thy clemency!"
Thou dar'st not think it, narrow ignorant soul?
But He, who saw the whole
In torture of that sweat
On bloody Olivet,—
Can'st thou beweep thy little misery,
And dull to His unthinkable sorrow be?
Weep for thyself?—No! till thine eyes were dim,
Knew'st thou the all, would'st sit and weep for Him!
I swear, were man not impotent as fell,
God were more sore in Heaven, than Satan in his hell!

## *DORMIAM ET REQUIESCAM*

Well, I am peaceful, with the pitiless Peace
That sits beneath the surface-seas of pain;
And the great roll and refluence of those seas
Shakes overhead, yet cannot shake her reign.

There is no more to say; I am at peace:
At peace—O iterate that slow curfew-bell!
For should its slumberous monody once cease,
This Peace might stir, and find her Queen of Hell.

## [THE JOY OF LIFE AND DEATH]

The joy of life? There is no joy in life;
The only joy, believe me, is in death.
Not the mere surrender from the world's mad strife,
The gracious yielding of ungracious breath.
Nay, but that death which is dull life's reward,
The blossom-fall which seeds the after-flower,
Which all the arduous cycle circled t'ward,—
This is the death which does death's self devour.
The joy to live choose he who will, not I:
Give for my part and boon the joy to die.

## [PATMORE AND *NEW POEMS*]

Take thou this book!
Thou didst not read it, living, O my dear!
Take it then, dead. My Judge, who only knew
Thereof the inmost true:
But now that inmost voice is none to hear.
That voice which, too late coming, found—thy bier.
It turneth a dumb look
On men of a strange language, most forsook,
And babbles a vain thing,
An isolate speech, no man interpreting.
O writ for thee, who wouldst not stay to hear,
Be then this book
A secret 'twixt my soul and thy dead ear!

## [LINES ON PATMORE'S DEATH I]

Leader of Song! thy truncheon sways no more
Song's chosen few; and me thou leavest here,
Who strove beside thee with unequal steps:
Unequal faltered by thee all the age,

And for great, greatness did not know thee great.
Some, with the archangel of our English quire,
Milton, and the half-legendary name
Of old Pythagoras, consenting say;
The music of the ever-moving spheres,
For dreadful bass and extreme vastitude,
Is to our ear's small round inaudible,
Too loud for man to hear. So, Titan, thou,
And motion of thy planetary mind
Thundered thine hearers deaf: they could not hark
Thy universal harmonies interwheel
Their paces, like the silent-footed heavens.
Men's wings dropped baffled down thy steep chasm
of song.

Not all the rhyme
That frets the reedy levels of the day,
Can fill the after-hollow of thy song,
And that loud pause ensuent, which doth the ear
Oppress like thunder. Therefore come I not,
No not, by all that renouncing bond
Which was the basic silence of our love,
To brag a grief above a new-made grave,
Set thy death-rattle to chiming verse, and make
My periods turn like worms about the tomb,
In the dead lion build my honeycomb,
And from the strong bring forth my feebleness.
No, for this thing the world grows dark—the great
Is dead, and all the little are alive!

## [LINES ON PATMORE'S DEATH II]

Gone. All the tender household amity,
Broken by Ill, Fate, Circumstance, and Pain,
Which was not, and shall not be knit again;
And thou, a sea-bird of the unknown main,
Passest the beacon of the loneliest star
Girt with the uttermost immensity.

Where thou go'st, say that I come soon. A space
Is yet for terribleness of some last ways,
Set, like my fate, beyond the regular
And comfortable paths of happy men;
And then—
The fatallest bottom where the fatal sand
Draws down to doom the scorners of the land,
And the sea's children perish by the sea.

## [LINES ON PATMORE'S DEATH III]

He spake my speech.
In all the world, he only.
He is gone
Beyond the utmost sun's most utmost reach,
And me he leaveth very lonely,
Being most like to one
That standeth sole upon an alien beach,
And sees the last sail of his kindred go
Down the horizon sinking slow;
Then, for his lids are stung
With tears, turns blinded to the unamicable land,
Wherein henceforth for ever shall no man under-
stand
His mother's milky and kiss-sweetened tongue.

Comfort me not;
For sorrow yet is young;
Let be, lest by your words she should be taught
The miseries
She is.
Have done, ye wrong her all!
Being a little grown,
And come to perfect moan,
She then shall know
How rich she is in woe,
Her hoarded tears shall be her own,
Which she shall spend with eyes most prodigal.

## ["GOD! IF THOU SITT'ST IN HEAVEN"]

God! if Thou sitt'st in Heaven, and judgest things below,
Sterner will be Thy measure, for Thou measurest slow;
To each coward Land whose appetite for gold or soil has thrust
Its sons forth to the torture and its daughters forth to lust,
Thou wilt apportion that sole scourge which it can feel—
Its gold to utter loss, its soil to the foreign heel,
While Famine with her sister Plague glean what is spared by
steel.

## [ENGLAND, OLD AND NEW]

If ever an envious Europe banded to buffet you,
Would not the heart of the England Old cry: "Lay our guns
by the England New"?
Yea, and against the leagued world roar the iron wrath of
the Saxon Two!

Our glorious daughter! thou, so like the mother in all,
That very likeness of likeness makes us jar and strive;
Is it for ever to be, the wrath inaugural,
Begun when Cornwallis yielded his red-coats up alive?
Is it for ever to be, the fleer, the illiberal taunt,
The "braggart, tyrannous" mother, the "tall-talked, upstart"
child?
The ghastly ghosts of rotting vituperation which haunt
Them that should be as mother and daughter, lovely and
mild?

'Tis a scornful sound to you when we haggle for pitiful trade;
'Tis a hateful sound to us when the bray of the dollar-licker
is brayed:
But be you right or be you wrong, our heart is flame on our
lips
When the cry of a war-worn people fans the fires of your
battle-ships.

Oh, then we know you are ours, and the motions of our womb
Are woman t'wards the magnificent child that shall wax when England wanes to her tomb!

Your nation's god the Dollar to the world you have proclaimed;
And if all the world believe you, you are surely self-defamed:
But ah, nor once nor twice, in no uncertain strains,
You have shown us what high heat throbs in your noble veins.

## *FUIT*

Where is the Land that bayed of old
The swaggering galleons off the main:
And from her sea-rock kennel growled
The leaguèd sail of France and Spain?
Where may that valiant Islet stand?
England, my Fair! thou art the Land.

Where is that Country, she, O she
Whose nostril took as breath o' the rose
The cannon-smoke? who held in fee
Tempest to hound upon her foes?
Where may that haughty Islet stand?
England, my joy! thou art the Land.

Where is the Land who nations shook
At bristling of her mane of steel?
Scattered, with bending of her look,
The snarling hatreds from her heel?
O palsied heart and potent hand!
Thou art—no, no—thou wert the Land!

But now, thou Crassus, whose palled mouth
  Nought savoureth but thy shameful gold,
Seek thee out where, of North or South,
  Is fearful safety bought and sold:
Seek thee it out, and pay down tame
The usury of thy years of fame.

Pay down each splendid deathly field
  From Frank or Russian ravished; well
May the proud nations somewhat yield
  To raze these from their chronicle.
Cringe thy loosed knee, and whisper low:—
"Not we did work your overthrow!

"How should we, we, who take your scoff,
  Your taunt, your spit, your muttered curse;
And as we wipe the spittle off,
  Chuckle, for ye have left our purse!
*We* stir uncivil broils? God wot
It was our fathers; blame us not!

"We, shaking Europe with the din
  Of rattled money-bags; we, whose lip
The heroic sound is versant in
  Of shares and consols, stock and scrip.
We, born of Albion strumpetted,
The wrong side of her ocean-bed.

"New Danaë of a scornèd kind,
  She wived green Neptune in her hour;
But, late grown wise, has come to find
  Best procreance in the golden shower.
And we, the pledges of her love,
Know but for god that sallow Jove."

So truck the fame would light a heart
  Beneath the scored hide of the Copt;
And take a license for thy mart,
  And grow thine oak—a little topped.
Go, go; home to thy huggèd ease,
And crouch behind thy whimpering seas!

Fallen mother, go; thy flaccid breast
  I writhe the mouth at: 'tis no fount
To suckle of song's sons the least
  Who hears the clang from Crécy mount.
Pulse thy lascivious timbrels! I
Banish me to the adopted sky.

Yet—if thou knew'st, in this thy day,
  What fits thy glory! Ah, for once
We loved thee! rouse, and to the fray
  Sad, last, and stateliest, wake thy sons.
Thou shalt not conquer, canst not fly;
But thou hast mighty ways to die.

Let Carthage teach thee. She, at least,
  Leaped on the throat o' the Roman foe;
Who, risen from under the struck beast,
  Knew scarce if he had scaped or no.
This way is thine, before they set
The stakes, and stab thee in their net.

Thou wilt not! Thy Dalilahs gloze:—
  "Sleep; for thou oft hast slumbered deep,
Yet, with the inrush of thy foes,
  Burst from their bands; thou therefore sleep."
The Philistines are on thee! shorn
Thy puissant locks, thou common scorn!

## [*VICTORIA REGINA, IN MEMORIAM*]

Now the bright lord of interlunar day
Plashes precipitous in the spattering East;
As a young Boy, in temerarious play,
Within his saponaceous laver small,
Whenas he looketh least,
Toppling descends in unprevisioned fall:
Wide through the room
And to the rafters flies the flecking spume.

(My use and customed style 'tis to begin
My strain inaugural
With orient allusion, though therein
Naught to my theme pertain.) O vidual
And lonely nation, that didst sit apart,
And hark the drip of tears within thy heart,
This is the cycle of that funeral
And empty day, when the disusèd crown,
Untenanted by august brows, cast down,
All Europe heard and mourned.
The power two-horned
Of either America, the South and North;
And the Pacific calms;
Veiled Asia sent the lamentation forth
To Africa, which beat her swarthy palms
Nor asked her Nile for waters. Austral eyes
To the imperial Russia rained replies,
Who thawed her steppes with tears. So dark a day
Full-circle comes this way,
To mind thee of a grief scarce dry,
And bid thee hallow a late-breathèd sigh,
While in a solemn rite
The stolèd priests unite,
And orisons the holy organs play.

Make your prayers for her; and bless her,
For the legend left to her successor;
For the precedent of rule
That has set the world to school;
For all she was, incorporate
With the wide form and body of the State,
A precept and a precedent
With daily use of Empire blent;
Not dead, but living pulse and part
Of England's regulated heart;
For these large habitudes of empire, yea
Half-conscious majesties of sway,
Which as by stealth
She taught her child, the Commonwealth;

For the responsive girth
Of English heart-beats round about the earth;
For these things, as we pray,
Render we thanks to-day.

Where she rests in quiet earth
May no cannon from afar
Bruit to her of foreign war:
Only the organ peal to her
The tidings of a nation's prayer;
Let this be the sole sound fretting
Her ear, that tells a people unforgetting,
And England kneeling round her sepulchre.

## THE SCHOOLMASTER FOR GOD

The devil girned as he lurched his hoof
  Over the border-wall,
The border-wall of the guarded garth
  That is God's garth withal,
The guarded garth where the trees of God
  Grew seemly fair and tall.

He soused the print of a cloven dint
  On the sod beneath him kneaden;
He crunched the scent from a lily-flower
  In the lily-ranks of Eden,
And tare the fruitage from the tree,
  Whatso was fairest seeden.

He filled his claw; on his writhen mouth
  A smile played wry accord;
As he leaped out of the Eden-close
  He neighed against the Lord:—
"I trow the hint of a slit hoof-print,
  Upon this trim-kept sward,
Right plainly shows your wingèd fellows
  Have kept but evil ward!"

That tale was told the Master
  Ere Satan had well leaped in,
And hot-plumed came the messengers
  To bruit the later sin.
Said Uriel: "Shall we bring him Thee,
  Haled hither by the chin?"
But Michael thumbed his lance's point,
  And stirred with armèd din.

The Lord made answer slow, as for
  Affair of little worth:
"Small luck has he with Eden-fruit,
  This robber from the North;
'Twas with My will that he brake in,
  With mine let him break forth."

The devil had face like a twisted thing
  As to earth with the spoil sped he;
And sowed the seed in a plot of his own,
  Where no blest foot might be,
And fostered it fast with his own mouth's blast,
  And watered it Stygianly.

Then he summoned the famished sons of men
  To fruit of Paradise:
"Now feed ye of each Eden tree,
  But and you pay my price,
And see that ye do me homage due,
  Who make the fruit to rise."

And he hath cried to blinded men:
  "Hither to me, to me!
O come, ye weary, woeful souls
  That thirst and languor dree;
Come and drink comfort, O drink deep
  From mine enjuicèd tree!

"This is the fruit of Paradise
  Desirèd from the first;
O eat the fruit of Paradise
  Long lost to man accurst!
Be not an-hungered any more,
  Nor any more athirst!"

The fruit thereof is fair and fine,
  And golden of its blee,
That well the Sons of God might think
  It came of Paradise-tree,
Nor deem how its root with cold Pit-fire
  Is suckled evilly.

The earthlings throng with greedy mouth
  To eat of that ill root;
For the Devil has gotten his criers out
  To cry the Eden-fruit.
Lord God, except Thou lift Thine arm
  Needs must be foul ensuit.

They ate the fruit, whose heavenly root
  Twined in Avernian sod;
And an unsated hunger scourged
  The eater with its rod,
Which might not be appeased—for they
  An-hungered were of God.

And some to the devil for comfort came,
  Who them did fatly dine
Upon his remainder-store of the husks
  Which the Prodigal ate with swine;
From fruit to husk, and husk to fruit,
  Went others—but to pine.

Yet one by one, and more and more
  (The noblest, leading those),
Drawn by that Eden-hunger sought
  The Master of the close;
For He alone could sate them, in
  Whose garth the first fruit grows.

*The devil groaned in himself and said:*
"I shall finish where I began:
I toil and toil, and I take in the end
But the sorriest clots of man;
Must I ever house at last in the swine,
On the filthy Gadarene plan?

"Like Peter, a fisher of men, sometimes
A man to my stomach I gain;
But the most are stuff that neither stamp
Of hell or heaven retain,
And for one that gives him his due, ten take
The devil's name in vain."

But the Master said: "Peace, Satan; still
I reap where thou hast sowed:
Still steal my truth, for truth like fire
Must tend back whence it flowed;
Despite himself, the devil must be
The schoolmaster for God."

## THE LILY MAIDEN

(*Sir Tristram, riding by a lake, meeteth a lily-crowned maiden, distraught by reason of her love's desertion; and she lamenteth her enforced virginity.*)

I have drunk of the lily's chalice,
Fed on snow of the thawless valleys;
In my cheek, since I drained the chalice,
Roses wither and lilies grow.
Heed you not if my thin cheek pale is,
Death's foot now in this lonely vale is;
Paler must wax my cheek that pale is,
Ere the rose in that cheek can blow.

Love has taken my heart from out me,
False love has girdled these snows about me,
How can I, with my heart from out me,
  Feed the flowers of my cheek to grow?
Cold is the snow of the thawless valleys,
Chill as death is the lily's chalice,
Only she who *seeks* the valleys
  Groweth roses amid the snow.

Fair, oh fair, is the land of lilies,
Gold is my new love as daffodillies,
Wingèd he walketh in heaven's lilies,
  And beckons his bride beneath the sod:
Mighty the rush of his tressèd rays is,
Vast the vault of the wings he raises;
He'll take my heart like a vase of praises,
  And break it over the feet of God!

## IN THE GARDEN

(A *Chanson*)

In the light of an odorous garden
  (Make merry, my heart in my breast!)
There is a pansy growing so dark
  With its heart of fire at rest.
    (Therefore shall we be merry?
    Make merry, my heart in my breast!)

In the light of a vaporous garden
  (Make merry, my heart in my breast)
There is a lady walking so sweet
  With her heart of love at rest.
    (Therefore shall we be merry?
    Make merry, my heart in my breast!)

In the light of a golden garden
  (Make merry, my heart in my breast!)
Flower and maiden are growing for me!
  (Bring hither the twigs to the nest!)
    (Therefore shall we be merry?
      Make merry, my heart in my breast!)

In the light of a saddening garden
  (Make merry, my heart in my breast!)
Why does the pansy lie bruised and dead,
  Unless by a footfall pressed?
    (Therefore shall we be merry?
      Hush, hush, my heart in my breast!)

In the sad of a sunset garden
  (O heart, O heart in my breast!)
What is the shadow that twins her walk,
  And are two black in the West?
    (Therefore shall we be merry?
  Let all the world be merry, but we
      Not more, my heart in my breast!)

## A BALLAD OF FAIR WEATHER

They went by the greenwood,
  The sunny-built forest,
They went by the water
  With hearts of the sorest;
They sought through the branches
  Entangled together,
The fern and the bracken
  A-flush in full feather
For death in fair weather.

They looked in the deep grass
  Where it was deepest;
They looked down the steep bank
  Where it was steepest;

But under the bruisèd fern
  Crushed in its feather
The head and the body
  Were lying together,—
Ah, death of fair weather!

"Tell me, thou perished head,
  What hand could sever thee?
Was it thy cruel sire
  Menacing ever thee?
Was it thy step-mother
  (Bird of ill-feather!)
Snapping the stem and flower
  Hid them together,
To soil thus fair weather?"

"My evil step-mother,
  So witch-like in wish,
She caught all my pretty blood
  Up in a dish:
She took out my heart
  For a ghoul-meal together;
But peaceful my body lies
  In the fern-feather,
For now is fair weather.

"My father, too cruel,
  Would scorn me and beat me;
My wicked step-mother
  Would take me and eat me;
My sweet little sister
  Will weep through the heather,
Not knowing, down there
  'Mid your clouds of dull feather,
That death brings fair weather.

"But I joy me most wishful,
  Desireless to range else,
Up here in the beautiful
  Land of the angels;
The beautiful angels,
  All laughing together,
Fan me to sleep
  With a gale of gold feather:
Ah, death brings fair weather!"

They have planted two willows
  To kiss one another
Where the sweet sister
  Kisses her brother:
The silver-drooped willows
  They mingled their feather
Where they are lying
  In sunshine together,
Asleep in fair weather,—
Dead, in fair weather.

## [THE TRAIN]

[In] baleful, belching smoky wrath,
The very devil of the scene,
The thunderous horror of the train,
Rushes its iron and ruthless way amain,
A pauseless, black Necessity.
Along its iron and predestined path
Treading out clangours, on the air
Fuming from its wide nostril smoke a-flare,
Tearing the night, an iron Destiny
Comes up dilating on its fore-pathed way.
No bands can hold it, and no mandate stay,
Nor the vast-ribbèd mammoth's rush abide
Touch of its plated hide.
Lo, jetting furious spark
Into the whirlèd dark,

It passes on its sombre-purposed track,
And the unsettled darkness surges slowly back,
The furrowed silence closes up behind.

## HORACE'S ODE ON LYCE

The gods have hearkened, Lyce, to my prayer,
The gods have hearkened, Lyce—you are old!
And yet you would be young,
And dally in wanton cups,

And woo with quavering voice the tardy Love.
But he his watches keeps in Chia's cheek,
Who sings, and blooms, and springs
Her stringed psalterion.

He taketh, restless boy, he taketh flight
From withered oaks, and wingeth flight from thee,
Shuddering at tarnished smiles,
Wrinkles, and blanchèd hair.

For purple brings not back the vanished years,
Nor any light of jewels brings them back,
Whom once the wingèd day
Hath calendared in Time.

Whereto has fled your beauty? Ah, whereto
Your rose, your fluent grace? Where is she, she,
Who stole me from myself,
Whose breath was breathèd loves;

She little lowlier blest than Cinara,
She with that countenance of winning wiles?
But fate to Cinara
Allotted fleeting years,

And Lyce kept co-rival with the crow,
That laughing youths with frequent coming view,
The torch of festival
Set into cindered ash.

# LIGHT VERSE

## [THE POET JESTER]

Paul (*viz.,* Oom) in patter
  You have here;
And that's the kind of chatter
  Folk hold dear.
I patter, patter, patter
Of Paul and Pauline matter,
And that's the kind of clatter
  Sends us sheer
Crazy as a cross between a March Hare and a Hatter.

The jester's bells I don
  (Something new);
My poet's robe is gone
  (Strange and true!)
Peter, Paul, and John
In the Bible they are one,
But in these days Paul and John
  They are two;
And that's the little quarrel that these verses turn
    upon.

Hear me shake my cap and bells!
  "Ah!" you say,
"We expected something else
  From his lay!"
Must one *always* work nought else
Than the high phantastic spells?
I think the record tells
  Phantastic, gay,
Are blent in Henley, Stevenson, and twin-accom-
    plished Wells!

## THE LARGER HOPE

Brown, from the loins of Philistines,
For six days laboured at his sins,
And rested from his labours one day,
And, to please Heaven, wore black o' Sunday;
Sinned, but in proper time and place,
And kept official hours of grace;
Drabbed, swore, in decent due degree,
Was drunk, but with sobriety;
Made of his sins no vulgar rumpus,
But profligate by chart and compass,
And, just as all good citizens are,
Most regularly irregular;
Lackeyed with vices, if you please,
But in respectable liveries,
All trained to know their proper places,
Nor call a blush to neighbours' faces;
To that well-wearing sort confined,
That steady, household, standard kind,
Which, bless your soul, can never hurt you,
And make France envy British virtue.
Brown was, in fact, no better or worse
Than others, so consent avers,
And never sinned beyond his purse.
So, not too proud to keep the pen,
And be d—d just like other men,
This fellow took the vulgar bent,
And went to hell by precedent.
"For if," thought he, "as preachers tell us,
The great, and rich, and prime good fellows,
Are mostly coal for nether bellows,
The devil, as it seems to me,
Has all the best society."

Thus, treading the swept way t'ward hell,
Upon the door of Heaven he fell;
The door flew open—in a trice
Brown blundered into Paradise.

He bowed, backed, blushed, quite overcome,—
Did not precisely feel at home;
Indeed to say truth, by your grace,
He had easier felt in t'other place.
Profuse apologies and sore,
But—Faith, he had mistook the door.
"No, not at all; come in, come in:
Kipling will tell you, vain is sin.
In Heaven we keep open house,
And never turn away a mouse:
Place, there, among the seraphim!
And—give him tune of the next hymn."
Brown, having to the throne salaamed,
By angels hymned, and angels psalmed,
Soft whistled: "Saved?—Well, I *am* d—d!"

## "THE VOICE OF THE TURTLE IS HEARD IN OUR LAND"

(*Hommage à M. de Rougemont*)

It was the gallant Waterton,
'Way down 'bout the Equator,
That witched the world with horsemanship
Upon an alligator.

'Twas the more brave de Rougemont
(Unless our ears he dupe)
That proved the turtle makes a steed,
As well as makes a soup.

I asked a turtle; he replied:—
"Green is my soup, I ween;
But in this case, my friend, 'tis not
The turtle that is green!

"Swallow, my friend, the turtle-soup,
  It will thee much avail;
Swallow, my friend, the turtle-soup,
  But not the turtle-tale.

"Though not for tails are turtles famed,
  Yet is it plain enough
Here is a turtle with a tale,
  And it is very tough.

"And though a turtle be no fish,
  'Tis proved and cannot fail
That here you have a turtle with
  A very fishy tale."

Now thanks to thee, my turtle friend,
  For the lesson thou hast taught!—
Though fish are captured by the mouth,
  Men by the *tale* are caught!

## GOING TO SCHOOL

(What a Boy Thinks)

In winter-time, in frost and rime,
  They pull me out of bed,
  From my snug little bed;
And off to school I have to go,
  Though cold winds blow,
And my ears tingle, and although
  My little nose is red.
I rise up in the morning
  To work the whole long day,
The whole long day at nasty books,
  When I'd much sooner play.

Now, if I had a little boy,
  I know what I would do,
  Yes, I know what I'd do.
I would not spoil his happy joy,

*My* little boy;
I'd let him stop with game and toy,
Not ask how much he knew.
He'd lie in bed in the morning,
Amuse himself all day;
And if they gave him nasty books
(*Such* nasty books!)
I'd pitch them all away!

And if they said: "Your little boy
His lessons never knows;"
I'd say: "*My* boy no lessons wants;
For when he taller grows,
He's going to be a soldier,
A big long sword to wear,
And thrash the Prussians and kill the Russians,
And show the French he will not blench,
For them he does not care;
Oh no!
For the French he does not care!"

# THE POET AND POETRY

## ["I SHOWED TO ALL MY GOODLY FRUIT"]

I showed to all my goodly fruit, my fruit of Paradise,
Like the new-washèd morning star, nor any man them buys.
Another came, for load who bare scooped husk and store of rind,
Thereat all sware such dainty ware was greatly to their mind.
"Here is marvel!" quoth I; "some spell is thine, or lucky star."
"No miracle!" said he; "I sell them, friend, Things as they Are."

## ON A REVIEWER, CALLING MY POETRY "AMBITIOUS"

It is ambitious—the grand style
   Or nothing, Mr. Reviewer!
Yet the wise gods do sometimes smile
   When critics are cock-sure.

If you, 'tis like, ambition see
   In yonder rising pine,
And if your grape ambitious be
   About its brand of wine;

Pactolus swell with bosom high,
   To mass his golden pile;
And your rose be ambitious, aye,
   To blow in the grand style;

Even as their effort, so is mine,
   And you are clearly right.
Ambitious stars! how shine
   Their efforts, thinks the night.

If the bird brave the perilous sky
   Applause and watch to wile;
If the bird brave the heavens, to try
   Its "daring" (save the while!)

I never yet to think did pause
   Were my song high or low;
And I attempt the sky because
   My pinions bear me so.

For me the labour were indeed
   To keep the goodly ground;
And then I move with lightest heed
   In the serene profound.

Why wilt thou think all spirits planned
   To sample of thine own?
And wilt thou give the cloud a band
   And bind it to the stone?

And dost thou think that lust of fame
   Alone attempts the skies?
And is there any pride in flame
   That does but simply rise?

I reason not of depth or height,—
   Let this for critics be!
I know but, where is my delight
   There is my liberty.

## [NO SINGER OF HIS TIME]

Ye have denied
Ye have denied
Ye have denied
Ye have denied
Nothing at all is of august and high,
Allaying man's dull dust, ye not deny:

Ye have said: "Go out from us, and leave our earth
Utterly of the comfortable clay;
Demand nought from us; let us hood our eyes
With a strong veil of flesh, for this is wise,
And but to peer forth is to pall in mirth;
Disconsolate and hateful is your day.
Your sights but trouble us: here in the mire,
Hognuts we have, if hognuts we desire;
Forth! for all comfort is in the fat clay
Whence man was dug in his ignoble birth,
And all disaster is it thence to stray."
Though sole and single be my wayfaring,
I will not be partaker of this thing.
Wherefore ye cry: "No singer of his time,
Not of to-day, nor yet of any day,
He shapes aloof an ineffectual rhyme,
Nourished upon the husks of threshed-out things,
Which who will harken? Of our fire-new world
No note has he. Pity! the man has wings,
But all as one it were that they were furled.
His muse he will not tire
Upon the entrails of the unclean ideals
Which serve for us;
His dainty Pegasus
Disdains nutritious hogwash. Still he flings
His aimless flight in —— gyre,
With some fool's dream of fleshless hymeneals:—
A Bee of Maeterlinck! 'Tis a waste lyre."

But you, not I, have strayed; but you, not I,
Have wandered from the mighty company,
Processional
Down the unshaken ages, testifying
To that which smiles at your most vain denying,
And stands though you must fall:
Yea, though the whole world with one tongue deny,
Answers: "Yet here am I!"

## [DEEPLY-SINNING MAN]

Ah, deeply-sinning man!
Thus to himself began
A Poet! "If the whole world could but know
Thee as thyself thyself dost know,
Would it not shun
And stop the nose at thee, dead carrion?
But oh!
I know the lofty mood,
The inner beauty, the desire
For heavenly clearness of beatitude,
The self-devotion to God's trampling feet,
His clement and vindictive tread of fire;
The circumstance which did
Thwart and forbid
The blossom's native spiring towards its small
Desired, uncompassed, individual
Fairness, by the shrill beat
Mournfully incomplete
Of hail, and frost that bites, and heat that sears,
And the refusèd fostering of the unequal years;
Unto myself am I
Immaculate wish hid with a maculate lie."
So did I in my mind
Pretend myself one self-deceived,
With art disguising art;
But the great Sire
Whose eye, although it shrived,
Was not thereby
Made blind,
Nor weakened of its ire,
Wrote with His finger in my dusty heart;
I read, and knew me Liar.

## A PASSING SONG

A nightingale upon a bough
  Sang the rose below:
A song upon a poet's mouth
  His love sang low.

When the rose is witherèd
  What shall fall the nightingale?
Or the song of the singer's mouth,
  Seeing love's frail?

The bird lay broken by the rose.
  Deathless sang and loftier-free
On the poet's mouth the song,
  Fed with agony.

This song, when the glittering cloud
  Resolved, nor ever was again
That glittering cloud; I overheard
  Sing in the rain.

## ["THE WATER TO THE STAR RETURNS"]

The water to the star returns, ah me!
His fainter self for guerdon sole and meet;
The tender flower has from the suckled bee
Only its own wild overplus of sweet;
The poet in his heart's great solitude
With his redundant song must be content;
And God, for all His vast o'er-tender mood,
Must count it much if men thereto consent.
  Small hearts by mighty longings are reproved,
  And the great love is ever least beloved.

## [A FOOL BY NATURE AND BY ART]

Yet must not envy scant deservèd fame,
But own his poems high and rare—like game.
Nay, this alone were prodigal nature's plan;
Behold the Artist supplement the Man!
In the small line, with dainty exquisiteness
Of feeble polish, polished feebleness,
Wrought and perfected till each vein concealed
Of native weakness is with skill revealed,
Learn thou the truth he can so well impart:—
*A fool by nature, is twice fool by art.*

## ["O FAIR AND AFFLUENT SABBATH OF MY MUSE"]

O fair and affluent sabbath of my Muse,
Ere yet I learned compelled humility!
When I could pause awhile from songful use,
And see the sweet creation good, nor sigh
As one who stints because the source runs dry—
A fountained nymph, whose lips are still a-stretch
In carven waiting for the wonted stream
Which no more shall her desolated mouth
Wet, though for ever she be stone and dream,
A wide-lipped figure of memorial drouth,
A derelict moon whose sun is in eclipse,
To customed glories—how beyond her fetch!—
Leaning from forth the sudden-happening dark,
The lampless newness, and the 'wildering chill.
Before that seeded doom had burst its husk,
That fate which waited threatening at the sill
Of my poor song advanced its shadow o'er
The threshold, and the long-expectant door
Beheld the apparition stand within;
Whereat the young songs huddled and were still,
And all unwarmèd were their roughening fans;

Oh, ere that figure made foreseen arrest
Upon the tender many-fledgèd din
Of my sweet household of yet-childling songs;
To you I gave my best,
When best was best indeed, nor were my vans
Feebled in flight by forecast of these wrongs.
For you were authors of that song indeed.
By you 'twas sheltered from the world's unheed.
You taught the song; and when I flagged to sing,
Yours was the cage whereto from wandering
Downward I sank, and closed my weary wing.
More than friends, second father, second mother,
To all succeeding days we live in one another;
No selfish ray can any of us shed,
But all must crown with light each other's head.
So blent our destinies, so blent our names,
We share our lives; yea, too, we share our fames!
For each within him felt the abundant life
Fit to portray colossal passions' strife.
To be ridiculous none feared, and thus
The few indeed were not ridiculous.
Each aimed full height; and, if he rose or fell,
Rose high as heaven, or sunk as low as hell.

## [A POET'S TESTAMENT]

My will? O heavy testament of void!
Which nothing has to leave in legacy
But that which it has not. My body even,
This dim disgrace of misconfided flesh,
I cannot will away: it is entailed
On the prodigal worm, its issue lineal,
That with succession indefeasible
Shall in my entrails kennel; nor shall hold
The ill-timbered lodging long. My poet's name?
Alack! upon what mart do congregate

The merchants that on such vain property
Will lend one moidore out; which is indeed
Not mine, but mortgaged for some sparsest pence
To the soon-foreclosing world. O nothing, nothing,
May this sad breath of mine behind me leave,
But some poor pleasances of word-enclosed
And much-toil-ordered thought; which they to come
Perchance shall pass as unregardfully
As those that in their daily multitudes
Pass by, unaware, occulted Paradise.

## A QUESTION

Wherefore should the singer sing,
  So his song be true?
Truth is ever old, old,
  Song ever new.

Ere the world was, was the lie,
  And the truth too:
But the old lie still is old,
  The old truth new.

# *PLAYS*

# NAPOLEON JUDGES

A Tragedy in Two Scenes

DRAMATIS PERSONÆ

NAPOLEON

GENERAL AUGEREAU: *Commanding a division in the French army.*

MADAME LEBRUN: *An Opera-dancer, Augereau's mistress.*

PRESIDENT OF THE COURT-MARTIAL

A FRENCH DESERTER

OFFICERS AND SOLDIERS

PLACE: Augereau's Camp

PERIOD: The Italian Campaign of 1796.

*During the first Scene,* NAPOLEON *is absent from Augereau's Camp.*

## SCENE I

Augereau's Tent. *A banquet in progress.* AUGEREAU, MADAME LEBRUN, OFFICERS.

MADAME LEBRUN. A conqueror, you? No, wine flies its red flag in your cheek; you are overthrown, general!

AUGEREAU. Wine?—That's love, my queen, love! That's the modesty of a French soldier, blushing to speak of his own exploits. When you have studied my sex so deeply as I have studied yours——

MADAME LEBRUN. The studies of General Augereau! [*Laughing.*]

AUGEREAU. I study war and women, war and women,—neat, that, *morbleu!*

MADAME LEBRUN. Oh, woman's heart is a volume that men diligently study,—granted, General! But it is as some of your soldiers study the newspapers,—because they are always hoping to find their own names there!

AN OFFICER. You are worse beset than by the Austrians, General!

A SECOND OFFICER. Why, an Austrian jest he can parry with the bayonet.

MADAME LEBRUN. Nay, and make sharp retort, too, I do not doubt: your sword, General, has a cutting irony, I fear.

SECOND OFFICER. Oh, Madame, we all wear a few feet of bright wit by our sides. [*Showing his sword.*]

MADAME LEBRUN. True, sir; and with you, that is the only wit which wine loosens: though you drink yourselves hot, your minds' wit keeps the scabbard.

AUGEREAU. You despise us, girl, you despise us: it is not a wise girl that mocks the thunder because it talks low to her.

MADAME LEBRUN. How? I mock?—Yes, if it talk and do me no service.

AUGEREAU. It will strike where you bid it, silly one.

MADAME LEBRUN. Will it? What would you give me indeed, if I asked you?—By this kiss, what?

AUGEREAU. All that is mine to give!

MADAME LEBRUN. What now?—Lose me a battle?

AUGEREAU. I had rather you bid me win you twenty. No, my battles are France's; those are not in my gift.

FIRST OFFICER. *Parbleu!* you would not ask him to run from the Austrians, Madame?

SECOND OFFICER. Or run *to* the Austrians, like the fellow that is to be shot to-morrow.

MADAME LEBRUN. Shot?

AUGEREAU. A deserter, pet; do not let him come between the wine and your lips.

MADAME LEBRUN [*with affected and hysterical levity*]. To-morrow? Are ladies admitted to the performance, General? I never saw a man shot.

AUGEREAU. What! a *Parisienne,* and never saw a man shot? Child of revolution, you have missed a pleasure.—Bring the fellow in and shoot him now!

FIRST OFFICER. General!

AUGEREAU [*in sudden fury*]. Aye! you, sir, who dare to "general" me, *you* bring the fellow in and shoot him! Quit the tent instantly, sir; take three of your company, bring the fellow in, and shoot him here.

SEVERAL OFFICERS. General, General!—You are drunk, General!

AUGEREAU. "Drunk, General," am I?—You insubordinate dogs, did you never see a general drunk before? What! am I commander here, and can I neither be drunk to please myself, nor shoot a scoundrel to please a lady?—Carry out your orders, sir; three of your company, bring him in, set him against the end of the tent, and shoot him here.

MADAME LEBRUN. Oh, my brave, I jested, only jested!

AUGEREAU. By Heaven, love, so do I,—jest, only jest; but when *I* jest, the muskets laugh in their throats!—Are you gone, sir? You know Augereau. [*Exit* FIRST OFFICER.]

MADAME LEBRUN [*laughing uneasily*]. You are terrible!

AUGEREAU. As battle! Ah, you see it is a lion you roll in those soft arms; they are mortal jaws that lick those little hands! Aha, aha, my love!

A THIRD OFFICER. But, General, this is only a joke, I hope; you will not carry it further?

AUGEREAU. No further than a musket will carry, I promise you. How! is he not sentenced? Is he not a deserter? He would not die like a soldier, for the sake of Mars: he shall die like a dog, for the sake of Venus. And too much honour! What can a poltroon of a deserter want? He shall have a glass of wine before he's shot, and a pretty girl to see him shot. Never a man I shot in my life died so sumptuously! [*Re-enter* OFFICER, *with* DESERTER *and three* SOLDIERS.] Good, you have obeyed. Set him right against the end of the tent,——

DESERTER. My officers, you will interfere for me! My sentence is for to-morrow. This is murder——

AUGEREAU. Ha! Is there any officer of mine will dare raise his voice against his commander's orders? Is there any guest of mine will incommode his host? Is there any Frenchman here will disoblige a lady?—Set him——

MADAME LEBRUN. Oh, this is no jest! This is frightful! For *my* sake, darling,——

AUGEREAU. It's for your sake I'm having him shot, my dear; all for your sake. Nay, don't cry—see, the miserable scoundrel is shivering! Would you keep a man like that in life, my dear? He's not fit to stand life. Here, give me that wine. [*To one of the officers.*] Kiss the glass, sweet.—Now you *shall* kiss it, I say; *morbleu!* you shall!—Nay, now don't cry into the wine: kisses are better than tears for a man that is going to be shot—or for a man that is not going to be shot, ha! ha!—Here, you cheesy-faced rogue, take off your wine with a kiss on top; and look down the muskets with some colour in your cheeks. Set him up against the end of the tent: so. Officer, give the signal. And you, fellows, do not disgrace the shooting of the French army before Madame. Give the signal, sir; you keep Madame waiting. If I have to do the thing myself, Madame is like to see two shootings instead of one.

OFFICER. Fire!

MADAME LEBRUN. Oh, God! [*They fire: the* DESERTER *falls. Horror.* MADAME LEBRUN *faints.*]

SECOND OFFICER. General, what have you done?

AUGEREAU. Done? Shot a deserter. Take away the body.

FIRST OFFICER. General, General, if Buonaparte were here!

AUGEREAU. Ha! what! Who dares say—"If Buonaparte were here"? [BUONAPARTE *enters unperceived.*] If Buonaparte were here, I would say—— [*Stops, seeing* BUONAPARTE.]

BUONAPARTE. Yes, General? Pray proceed, I am listening. "If Buonaparte were here, you would say——?" Go on. "If Buonaparte were here?"—Ah, General, if Buonaparte were here!

## SCENE II

The same Tent. *A court-martial sitting, with* AUGEREAU *before it, under guard.* MADAME LEBRUN, *the* OFFICERS *present in the last scene, and* SOLDIERS *guarding* AUGEREAU. *At the other side a banquet set out. Enter to them* NAPOLEON.

NAPOLEON. Is the finding of the court delivered?

PRESIDENT. It is.

NAPOLEON. And you find him——?

PRESIDENT. Guilty. According to your orders, we have reserved sentence for yourself.

NAPOLEON. You have done well. Sentence is for me. Let me look on this man. [*The* PRESIDENT *yields him his place.* NAPOLEON *gazes for a while at* AUGEREAU, *without speaking.*] Well, General! what have you to say? Silent?—Ah! you are silent now: better had you been silent *then!* You gave the order for that poor wretch's execution—you have given the order for your own! Not I, not I, but you! Miserable man! of what were you thinking when you sat down to that red repast?—Butchers wash their hands before they come to table; but you—you clasped your mistress with assassination on your hands, you dipped your morsels in the blood of a French soldier! You filled your cup at his veins, I tell you! Your light-o'-love asked the death of a man: I may thank her moderation it was not of an army. Would I know my very conquests safe? Henceforth I must pray that my generals' wantons bear a conscience in their love-demands. For one kiss you bestowed on her a murder! You banquet, you lip your paramour, while your men famish, with their sweethearts left among the corn of home:—that is not enough! To your epicurean dinner you must add a terrible dessert. You cannot savour your wine, without a relish of death. Your commander, when he enters your tent, must tread underfoot the waste leavings of humanity dropped from your table. Ah, you were in haste to sweep up that red remnant of the feast! By what right, I ask you, by what right, do you toss my soldiers' bodies, like superfluous fragments, among the broken viands that strew the floor of your carousals?

AUGEREAU. When you talk of discipline, you are my commander: when you talk of morality, you are not my priest. We have heard overmuch of the lady, General Buonaparte: did she embrace me? —her embraces left my sword-arm free! Let the enemies of France bear witness to it.

NAPOLEON. Am I the custodian of your morals? Not so. But when you take your Opera-Herodias from her fiddles and set her among the trumpets, to kiss men's deaths out of your lips lightly as the gold out of your purse; when my soldiers' sentences are decreed from the tribunal, but their execution decreed from the green-room; then, sir, I tell you that in this theatre of war there are no *coulisses*. Sir, sir, you have thrown costlier pearls in this woman's wine, than were ever dissolved in the Egyptian's vinegar! Two lives and an honour has she drunk up; and one life, like the honour, is your own. Morality? A lower than Heaven's State-Court will suffice to try *your* cause. I curb not your light loves: but keep time and place, General! keep time and place! It is public fornication to lie with her under the eagles of France, to wrap your concubinage in the flag of the Republic!

Think what this man has done to while away his empty hour: think, gentlemen; think, you whom I must call a general of the Army of Italy. You have follied with the terrors of the French arms! Leave your graves, leave your combats, Luxembourg, Vendôme, Condé, Turenne, Dumourier, Hoche, Pichegru,—all you splendours of Gallic war: with the muskets you used for victory, wanton wenches try how soldiers bleed, and fill with a death the gap between two yawns!

You have heard in evidence the whole story, Officers: too many of you saw it with your own eyes. The French soldier (for a soldier he was, if a guilty one) shot at the signal of a public commoner's laugh, kissed through the heart by a dancer, his blood mingling with the wine-smears of a lascivious banquet—— At what shudder you, gentlemen? Oh, you forget, sirs: these are love-toys that I tell you of!

Does Dubois envy you, General, think you? Dubois, who fell in that last battle where you had better have fallen. Better the dead on his couch of honour, than the living in the couch of a courtesan. Yet lie there if you will; I prevent you not: but make not the tricolour your coverlet! Ah, ah! what have you done?—You have given the laurels of Napoleon to your harlot for a plaything!

Once more, General. Have you any plea to stay sentence? Still silent? Then, judgment is recorded; for me remains sentence. All are present who witnessed the act? Gentlemen, you participated in a banquet and an execution. In a banquet and an execution you *shall* participate. Gentlemen all, take your seats. [*Sits at table. Some seat themselves; most remain standing in speechless consternation. Murmurs.*]

*Sit,* gentlemen! [*They seat themselves.*] Madame, here is your place. [*Pointing to the seat beside him.*] You beheld your last entertainment by the side of General Augereau. You will not disdain to behold *this* by the side of Napoleon? [*She is borne half-*

*fainting to the seat, turns to him with a piteous attempt at blandishment, and tries to speak, but fails.*]

Nay, Madame, *this* time you have no need to ask. Your request is anticipated. Captain, [*to the* OFFICER *who commanded the firing-party in the First Scene*] order in the three soldiers who provided the former amusement. After so excellent a rehearsal, I trust that Madame's little entertainment will now run smoothly. [*Exit* OFFICER.]

AUGEREAU. General, Justice I expect, to Justice I resign myself; but this is not Justice, this is vindictiveness, this is atrocity!

NAPOLEON. Atrocity? You may know something of *that:* but Justice? —Dear General Augereau, you have, I understand, "studied war and women"; but you have studied neither Justice nor Me. [*Re-enter* OFFICER, *with* SOLDIERS.] Quick, place the General at the end of the tent, and get your interlude over with despatch: Madame, I see, is impatient, and these gentlemen's curiosity somewhat mars their appetite. Let me exhort you, by the way, not to disgrace the shooting of the French army before Madame. [MADAME LEBRUN *breaks from his side, and throws herself at his feet.*]

MADAME LEBRUN. Mercy, mercy!

NAPOLEON. Aye, the harlot's mercy he shall have! Habitation of lust and death! he had better have stroked the sabre's edge than you, kissed the musket's mouth than yours! The sword sometimes spares, the musket sometimes misses; the harlot, never! Fair Destruction! he has clasped you a thought too close to his breast!

MADAME LEBRUN. Nay then, nay then, it is I who have clasped destruction to my breast! [*Draws a pistol from her bosom, and points it at herself.* NAPOLEON *wrests it from her.*] Oh, miserable girl! Oh, impotent girl! Thrust yourself before a wild beast, it will leave its prey and turn on you: it is not so, I find, with Death! He will not loose my love, to feed on me! Is it not enough, is it not enough, Conqueror, that you sentence *him* to death; must you sentence *me* to life?

NAPOLEON. Take her away. This woman's very gaze, I see, wrenches Justice from its course: Justice cannot work under her eye. Take her away.

MADAME LEBRUN. Let me stay, I demand to stay! I have borne your tortures, I have a right to see him die!

NAPOLEON [*stamping his foot*]. Out of the tent with her, quick! [*He lays the pistol on the table. As he does so, it goes off, and* MADAME LEBRUN *is struck between the arms of the* SOLDIERS.]

MADAME LEBRUN. Out of the world is quicker! See you, Little Corporal? You are strong indeed: Death, which scorned my bidding, comes to me at yours.

NAPOLEON. *Maledetta!* his destiny, or this woman, is mighty!

MADAME LEBRUN. Ah, you of many fights, you never before fought with love! I have loved aside your bullet!

NAPOLEON. Shoot him, if he moves a step! [*As* AUGEREAU *is about to rush to her side.*]

MADAME LEBRUN. Soldier of Destiny, listen to your goddess! Fate has made her own election, and it is I, not he. She who asked a death, has taken death: the guilty pays,—then spare, spare him! Pardon, pardon! [NAPOLEON *turns away his face.*] Pardon! Oh! hero, can you not love? then you can relent. Are you all hero? Is the god in your ancestry tempered with no pitiful mortality? Men say—say, you are—that the soul of the Roman Conqueror revisits earth in you. Then, re-born Caesar, remember Cleopatra!

NAPOLEON [*bending over her*]. Child, you are out in your part: Antony should have died for Cleopatra, not Cleopatra for Antony.

MADAME LEBRUN. Do I die in vain?

NAPOLEON. Truly, Death is a wonderful posture-master: you never danced before as you have danced this Dance of Death. They had tragic dancers of old:—none like you, none like you!

MADANE LEBRUN. I have made you weep!—Talma will never have such a triumph as that!

NAPOLEON. I weep for the accident of my fatal hand. *You* should have lived, girl, not he.

MADAME LEBRUN. No, do not weep: your hand has made death glorious; your tongue, I trust, will make death happy.

NAPOLEON. If it can—yes. Go, General, you have your lesson. When you fire such bullets at a soldier, they do not rest in his body: they pass through, and strike your loves. [AUGEREAU *springs to her side.*]

MADAME LEBRUN. Keep him, Caesar, to win your battles; for surely wounds will not touch him: I have taken his wounds upon me, and left him only the victories. [*To* AUGEREAU.] Ah, General! I have intercepted the stroke of Caesar. You said, General, they were mortal jaws which licked my hand:—alas! I find them so! Ah, General! [*Dies.*]

NAPOLEON [*to* AUGEREAU.] Man, man, I pity you! Not that you have lost her; but that, having her, you knew her no better than I have known her.—Cover the body. Come, gentlemen, come: if you have as little stomach as I, you are not for eating. We trespass here on Death's dark supper-chamber; he would be private. Come.

# MAN PROPOSES, BUT WOMAN DISPOSES

*Un Conte sans Raconteur*

In Two Scenes

### *APOLOGIA PRO FABULÂ MEÂ.*

Immemorially courteous, dear, and gentle Reader,—

Here is but one pennyworth of man to an intolerable deal of woman. For this the Author apologiseth, that in a provincial suburb one man to four women is a most excellent and accustomed proportion. And if, to say truth, the man is but man-and-water, for this also is there a reasonable colour. Woman (saith the poet) is to man, as water unto wine; and where the water is so plenty as in the suburbs foresaid,—faith, the wine perhaps is apt to get something diluted. Yet, for thy sake, would it were stronger! Of the converse wherein these gentle dames delight, I have ventured to put upon thee but one verisimilar ensample, and that too (as Cassio hath it) craftily qualified: the main interfeminine converse is near as artificial as eighteenth-century comedy, and was that way designed. I pray thee, think somewhat of this little piece; for I would fain think somewhat of thee. Thine, as thou usest him,

THE AUTHOR.

### PERSONS

MR. WILLIAM MORTIMER: *All the man the reader is like to get.*

MRS. HILLER: *A Widow (or thereabouts),* confidante *and intriguer to the neighbourhood.*

MISS BLACK
MISS BROWN
MISS WHITE
} *"Matter too soft a lasting mark to bear, And best distinguished by black, brown, or fair."*

A SERVANT

The CHARACTERS OF SEVERAL GENTLEMEN who do not otherwise appear.

PLACE: Aldham, one among the suburban districts of Alcester, a great provincial town.

## SCENE I

*The parlour of* Mrs. Hiller's House. MRS. HILLER *occupied with a morning-caller,* MISS WHITE. MISS BLACK, *another morning-caller, sitting by.*

MISS WHITE. Well, as I was going to tell you, Mr. Challen is engaged to Mary Fletcher.

MRS. HILLER. You don't say so! And he was considered such a catch!

MISS WHITE. Was? *Is!* There will be plenty of envy among the other girls. We have so few gentlemen, you know, in Tamerley, and he was *quite* one of the most agreeable. And—oh! I forgot! What do you think? George Hill is to be married to Lucy Poyntz.

MRS. HILLER. At last!

MISS WHITE. At *last,* dear! They had been engaged such a time, it was *quite* scandalous. And they say, you know—— [*One of those little scandals which the most unexceptionable ladies seem to like best.*]

MRS. HILLER. And when is the marriage to be?

MISS WHITE. In March. They are going away for it, and there are to be *no cards.*

MRS. HILLER. No cards!

MISS WHITE. No. Oh, it's quite the talk! I have seen her *trousseau,* —— [*An amazing paraphernalia of millinery, for which refer to the* Tamerley Tattler *of the time.*] And oh! I have another piece of news for you. Mr. Smoothman has accepted a call to a London chapel—I was told the name, but I forget it.

MRS. HILLER. I am *very* sorry. We shan't have him here any more, then. That will be another great loss to you.

MISS WHITE. Yes, a great loss. We all liked him so much. But he's sure to get on in London, he is *so* clever.

MRS. HILLER. If—if his good looks don't spoil him.

MISS WHITE. Oh, my dear, you don't know men! [MRS. HILLER *looks as if she thought she did.*] A man doesn't think of his looks.* There's no danger of that kind for men. A man is thought *nothing* of, I assure you, nothing at *all,* if he thinks of his looks. He's thought a *coxcomb.*

* This is an engaging trait in his own sex which the writer cannot say he has noticed. It is the more pleasing, therefore, to have it stated on such unimpeachable authority as that of the other sex.

MRS. HILLER. That's his portrait, Edith. [*Pushing it over to* MISS BLACK, *who studies it while the ladies chatter.*]

MISS BLACK [*sotto voce*]. Ah! wavy hair, careful curls, self-conscious insipidity,—made to stand in a pulpit, but not to open his mouth. If anybody were rash enough to think him a coxcomb, I fear—I fear—I should be rash enough to agree!—*Can* they do nothing but chitter-chatter? [*The ladies instantly disprove the rash surmise by proceeding to chatter-chitter. At length:—*]

MRS. HILLER. Well, if you *must* catch this train——

MISS WHITE. Oh, yes, I really must!

MRS. HILLER. Good-bye then, dear [*kiss*] dearest [*kiss*] Louisa! [*kiss*] Be *sure* to come and see me again soon.

MISS WHITE. As soon as I can *possibly* find time. Good-bye. [MRS. HILLER *accompanies* MISS WHITE *to the door.*]

MISS BLACK [*soliloquising*]. "Dear—dearest—Louisa!" What an adieu! An adieu parenthetical with osculations. Why, it is very kiss-sandwich, with endearments for bread-and-butter! Our sex are much to blame for depreciating the currency of kisses, and causing the stock of endearment to fall in the market. I have seen children be-loved and be-sweeted, till "sweet" was not sweet to them, nor "love" love. And I, when Annette comes back, shall begin to "my dear" her. To rail at a fashion and follow it is the way of Eve's daughters the world over,—nay, rather of Adam's brood. [*Re-enter* MRS. HILLER.]

MRS. HILLER. She always stops long, and always talks like that,—tiresome woman! And now, Edith, I have time to look at you. How *well* you are looking! It's an age since I've seen you, and I *particularly* wanted to have a chat with you, about—about—something. Now we can have it quietly. But first all you have to tell me about yourself. [*"All about yourself" the reader is spared.*] And now, Edith,—when are you going to get married?

MISS BLACK. *Can't* you talk about something else? I'm a little sick of this matrimonial gossip.

MRS. HILLER. I sympathise with you, my poor child. But it happens that just now I have a reason for "this matrimonial gossip."

MISS BLACK. That is an unexpected pleasure. It will be the first time I knew reason to have anything to do with it.

MRS. HILLER. Then answer to your interrogatory, Miss!

MISS. BLACK. Oh, you apostle of matrimony!

MRS. HILLER. It is the only apostolate licensed to women, my love; though I don't know why it should be. In many respects we should make very pretty apostles. If there be any truth in the libels on our sex, though we had not the Holy Ghost, we should at any rate have the gift of tongues. But you shall not put me from my question. Come, have you no eligible selection? You have plenty, you know, and it's time you chose.

MISS BLACK. Oh, yes; you know my list. It's every other girl's list. A girl here is like a guest at certain dinner-tables, where to accept an invitation to have anything is such transparent selfishness that all the other guests glare at you; and if you didn't refuse, there would be nothing left for the rest to look at. And if every girl here were to accept a helping to a husband—the result would be the same. "Shall I help you to a trifle of husband, Miss Black?" "No, thank you, I am not hungry; I've a very poor appetite."

MRS. HILLER [*laughing*]. Help yourself, my dear, and don't mind the other girls. It may teach our unbountiful host, Providence, to be less mean with the next generation. It *is* curious, though, how—with so many girls waiting to be served—the men go round and round untasted, like bad claret.

MISS BLACK. It is a miracle—the seven barley loaves with a difference. For alas! we are not all filled. The fact is, an eligible youth here is like the British detective—he can catch nobody because he is known to everybody. So he is passed from house to house like a fashionable novel in a circulating library, which all thumb but no-one buys: till, losing vogue a little, he falls out of demand, ceases to be inquired for, and is returned to the shelf.—Well, call the roll of possible suitors, Annette. They will not answer to their names, and I'll put black marks against all of them.

MRS. HILLER. Well, let me see; we must classify them, I think. What class shall we start with?—Place for literature!

MISS BLACK. Literature? Who is there?

MRS. HILLER. There's Mr. Joyce.

MISS BLACK. I wasn't aware he wrote. What has he done?

MRS. HILLER. He edited a "Browning for the Nursery," with appropriate explanations.

MISS BLACK. Ah, save me from the Browning commentators! One can only say with the lady in *The Critic*—"Here are two very civil gentlemen trying to make themselves understood, and I don't know which is the interpreter." And *what* did you say? "Browning for the Nursery"? Mercy on me! Would you have me marry King Herod?

MRS. HILLER. Well, it *might* be a preferable choice. Yet he is madly in love with you, Edith. He worships you as men do Heaven.

MISS BLACK. Truly, you mortify me. I never esteemed his worship much, but I did not think it had been so little as that.

MRS. HILLER. But he talks pretty well, don't you think? What do you think about his opinions on literary subjects—you, who reckon yourself some judge?

MISS BLACK. How mightily serious you are of a sudden!—I follow his own example, and don't think about them at all.

MRS. HILLER. But there seemed to *me* much thought in his opinions?

MISS BLACK. There is much opinion in his opinions—very little thought.

MRS. HILLER. You have not waited long to begin your black marks. Then there is Mr. Dearing, the linguist.

MISS BLACK. Doesn't answer to his name. Mark him down—a fool in seven languages. Insufficiency of mother-wit should find sufficiency in its mother-tongue. Proceed.

MRS. HILLER. Edith, Edith, take care; you are too sarcastic with that man in his own presence: you may provoke him to do you an ill turn.

MISS BLACK. You touch my anxiety: he has it in his power to do so, I confess.

MRS. HILLER. How?

MISS BLACK. He may make love to me.

MRS. HILLER. Nothing serious will come from you this morning. Then there is Mr. James, the poet. He sends you strictly secret poems. He is wiser in his generation than most children of light, he takes a sure way to publication.

MISS BLACK. Mr. James? Oh! my dear, he's a genius, they say, and might make an endurable husband, if one had the remotest surmise what he *is*. But he's the Arcane, the Unknowable, the—the——

MRS. HILLER. Edith!

MISS BLACK. My dear, he's an Occult Science. You have to be initiated into him like a Theosophy, or a Mahatma, or an Esoteric Buddhism, or whatever they call those dreadful things where you pass through ten Planes, you know, to see whether you'll prove a fool at the end of 'em. I've been three years a neophyte in Mr. James, and only reached the Second Plane.

MRS. HILLER. You ridiculous girl! And what is that?

MISS BLACK. Why, I'm admitted to his most confidential reticence. I'm more intimately ignorant of him than is any other woman. At that stage he writes me passionate poems, and when I meet him with a little interest, as a girl can't help having in a man who addresses her after that fashion,—and they really *are* beautiful poems, you know,——

MRS. HILLER. Being addressed to *you,* love, I can't doubt it.

MISS BLACK. Oh, thank you! [*Aside.*] I'm not sure whether I oughtn't to hate her for it, though! [*Aloud.*] Well, then he gazes gloomily into immense futurity, hardly notices me, and leaves me with a hand-shake that would turn a Mænad ice. And I think the wretch expects me to sympathise with him! I think he imagines that he is tacitly revealing to me his profound woes—what is it?—"the depths of his nature."

MRS. HILLER. Now, don't libel him, love. He doesn't talk like that.

MISS BLACK. Did I accuse him of talking at all? My dear, I'm not Stanley enough to explore this Hercynian forest of a man. And if I tracked his "hidden nature" to its source, I believe I should find it a rock-spring. I believe his Mystery is just—mystery. That's what most adepts find, don't they?

MRS. HILLER. It is supposed to be all the mystery of Theosophy, love. But, do you know, you paint to me a man who a little—interests me?

MISS BLACK. He interests you at first, a little, because he is so surprisingly uninteresting. But when you come to suspect that the reason he is so difficult to find out is because there is nothing to find out—! No; I don't mind discovering that he is an empty attic; but I dislike having to go up so many stairs to it. And I don't believe his poems, you know. I don't believe he means them—any more than he means himself. If I marry, and don't marry him, I believe he would write precisely the same to my baby, if he had no other object to address.—Next, please!

MRS. HILLER. Poor fellow! not his hearsay genius can keep you from setting your blackest mark.

MISS BLACK. Who?—I?—against his genius? No, dear, only a query against that. What! I'm half a genius myself: do you take me for the dull Roman in the play, that I should prick down my kindred in our proscription?

MRS. HILLER. It is the first I heard of the relationship, I promise you. What *faux pas* in the family of the Muses is responsible for it? *You* half a genius? Why half, why?

MISS BLACK. Oh, who is it, you know, says that "genius does what is right without knowing it"? And though I mayn't do what is right without knowing it, *en revanche* I often know what is right without doing it.

MRS. HILLER. Conceded: you go a long way towards genius. To our proscription, then, as you call it. Let me see, there are the doubtful characters we might take next.

MISS BLACK. Doubtful characters! Are there any? What a stimulating break in the monotony of our virtue!

MRS. HILLER. Edith, do you think that smart?

MISS BLACK. No, dear; merely natural. Virtue in Aldham is like temperance in the Sahara. Oh! for the wicked lover of the dead romantic days!—the man who broke hearts as if they were Commandments, and thought the Decalogue a beggarly allowance of sins for a gentleman. Indeed if you consider it, Annette, the Decalogue is primitive, too primitive: it might pass in the days of the golden calf—men whose stomachs could be faithful to one dish for life, a digestive monogamy of manna, might be content with a *repertoire* of ten transgressions; but the expanding peccatorial genius of the race demands an enlarged edition.

MRS. HILLER. *With several thousand additional sins, including all those in most modern and received usage,* like a revised Johnson's Dictionary? It is well Aldham does not hear you.

MISS BLACK. Oh, such a lover is a dream, only a bright dream! I know Caesar Borgia, in Aldham, could do nothing darker than smoke pipes in the drawing-room.

MRS. HILLER. Well, my doubtful people reduce themselves to one, and he is not Caesar Borgia;—Mr. Felton.

MISS BLACK. Oh, he's American, isn't he? He's not been long enough to do much here. He doesn't go to church, that's the worst I know of him. But proceed; I long to believe worse.

MRS. HILLER. So does Aldham.

MISS BLACK. And I will be as content as I may with something less than Caesar Borgia.

MRS. HILLER. You must needs. As you say, he has been too short a time here to have made himself a character; but he is charitably supposed to have several divorced wives in America.

MISS BLACK. Oh, that takes the romance off the thing! Romance parts with its gloss, where the powder falls on it from the wig of Law. If he'd several wives that he hadn't divorced, or several wives that he hadn't married—but this is *quite* unromantic. No, I don't think one could take a *divorcé* without a written character from his last situa—— I mean wife. Besides, I don't imagine, from what I have seen of him, that he can have real style in villainy, but should take him for an untutored genius. I can conceive him born with such natural capacity for evil, that his vices have not even the merit of cultivation. And I am not in his thoughts, dear. Were I his Maker, he could not think less of me.

MRS. HILLER. You have given him a very black mark, Edith. Well, we'll quit the students and the doubtful characters, and take the unprofessional men.

MISS BLACK. Thank you, I prefer them to the students. They have time to study being agreeable.

MRS. HILLER. What of Mr. Graham?

MISS BLACK. Oh! he says—he flatters himself he "knows women." When a man says he knows women, he means he has known bad ones. Won't do. Pass on.

MRS. HILLER. What do you say to Mr. Mortimer?

MISS BLACK. Why, only that he's something of a fool.

MRS. HILLER. Edith, your manners lack composure, to put it mildly. So does your judgment, to put it still more mildly. I want you to marry him.

MISS BLACK. Annette! your tactics aim at surprise, to put it mildly. Your conduct of them is a much greater surprise, to put it still more mildly. I can't marry him.

MRS. HILLER [*aside*]. Then she hasn't got John Cumberland's letter. I thought not. [*Aloud.*] Why?

MISS BLACK. Firstly, for the reason I have already given. Secondly,—surprise for surprise, Annette!—I'm engaged to Mr. Cumberland.

MRS. HILLER [*aside*]. You'd use the past tense, my love, if you knew the truth. [*Aloud.*] Edith!—and you have kept it from me!

MISS BLACK. I found the situation so new, and myself so shy.

MRS. HILLER [*aside*]. Then I think John has anticipated her a little, that's all. [*Aloud.*] You owe me reparation, dear. Make it. Marry Willie Mortimer.

MISS BLACK. Again!

MRS. HILLER. You refuse—let's see why. Firstly because he's, hypothetically, a fool. That doesn't matter, my love. Fools make imperfect lovers, I admit; but excellent husbands.

MISS BLACK. Stop this. I'm engaged.

MRS. HILLER. That doesn't matter either, dear. An engagement is a chain and collar, which holds your lover, according to law, but only holds you until you let go the chain.

MISS BLACK. Annette, I don't love him, and I love Jack.

MRS. HILLER. That doesn't matter either, sweetest. I didn't ask you to love him, I asked you to marry him. To desire love with marriage, is like expecting butter on your wedding-cake, my dear. Heaven works by compensations, and a woman shouldn't neglect the example of Heaven. To love one man and marry another—that's an equitable division of happiness, I take it.

MISS BLACK. Your ideas of love, and mine, are a little different, Annette. Plato——

MRS. HILLER. What is to be done with a girl that talks about Plato!

MISS BLACK. Oh, any girl may talk about Plato, provided she hasn't read him. Nay, in these Girton days girls may, if they choose, read the Ancient Fathers, like Mrs. Browning.

MRS. HILLER. My sweetest, women who love the Ancient Fathers are seldom loved by the youthful sons.

MISS BLACK. You're a cynical, hard-hearted——

MRS. HILLER. No, I'm not. Edith, you little goose, you don't love John Cumberland.

MISS BLACK. Annette, with your frivolous, worldly nature, you can't know the latent capacities of affection in my——

MRS. HILLER. O-o-oh!

MISS BLACK. Don't tap your shoe in that way! I tell you, you only see the sunlight on the pool; the depths——

MRS. HILLER. A-a-ah!

MISS BLACK. Annette, you are aggravating! The depths which it conceals——

MRS. HILLER. The sunlight or the pool? Is that his last poem to you?—the gentleman with the many pairs of stairs to his attic? You dear foolish girl, this boy (who *may* have depths, for all I know, but it's not deep in him to write of *you* like that) this boy has written poems to you till you begin to think yourself what he thinks you. You *like* young Cumberland; he's nice to play with, I dare say: but you're not made either for tragic misery or tragic happiness. You'll be decently happy with any man, if he's good to you, and doesn't interfere with you too much.

MISS BLACK. It's second-hand cynicism, Annette!

MRS. HILLER [*sotto voce*]. That's perhaps better than second-hand poetry.

MISS BLACK. To please you, you would have me break Jack's heart and my own.

MRS. HILLER. Oh, *dear* no! I shouldn't dream of such a suggestion! Why, what old fashion-book of the affections have you been studying? That is very high-waist-and-sandals in the history of emotional costume; we don't wear broken hearts at this end of the century. Mercy! what antiquated modes you would tie us to! That has gone out of vogue even in the provinces. Hearts don't break nowadays. They used to do, one reads, in one's grandmother's time; from which it is inferrable that our ancestors' hearts were of very inferior workmanship, and that the make of heart has greatly improved since their day. Then, I allow, even fine ladies' hearts would sometimes break if you threw 'em aside too carelessly; but now—Lord, child, a country-wench would have a better-made article. In these days the blessings of an unbreakable heart are open to the humblest.

MISS BLACK. You are detestable! You talk like an Englishman's Frenchwoman.

MRS. HILLER. France, the dear land whose literature rids us of our blushes, and whose invention sends us rouge to supply for them! Don't lay my views on its head even in that indirect fashion. They are native as an Englishwoman's style of lifting her skirts in a miry street. Listen to a little sense, child. Young Mortimer has money, and you're not made to do without money. He's good-looking; he's not a fool, as you say he is; he's read much what you've read, and he thinks about it not too much more than you do—which is an excellent thing. He won't be-goddess you, and you wouldn't like being be-goddessed for long. You would always be afraid that you were going to be found out, you know. That's why you don't like poor Mr. James. You're afraid of him, Edith. He wants to see you too close. He wants to come too near you. You're afraid of emotion and of deep things. If that merman once laid his arms round you, he would drag you down to his sea-weedy, inhuman caves, and you would die—or divorce. You want the air and the levels. You can't live in the deep, and he can't live on the surface. You are right to hold him aloof, though you don't know how right you are. Even Mr. Cumberland has a little too much of the under-waters for you. My man is the right one. Besides, [*looking at her like a surgeon about to make an incision*] you *must* have him, for I've offered him to Clara Gray, and she's refused him.

MISS BLACK. I wonder you dare to tell me so!

MRS. HILLER. Oh, you don't know how much I dare! You see, he loves both of you——

MISS BLACK. That is, neither.

MRS. HILLER. You don't know men if you think so. It's like—you know the pictures you see in shops? You stand on one side of the picture, and it is Salisbury; you stand in the middle of it, and it is Gladstone; you stand on the other side, and it is Churchill. From the picture learn a parable, and the way of a man's love. It all depends on the point of view. Willie Mortimer stands right of his heart, he sees Clara. He stands left of it, he sees you. I have only to fix him on the left side, and you become to all intents the sole occupant of that spacious tenement.

MISS BLACK. Annette, you take my breath away!

MRS. HILLER. I thought I should.

MISS BLACK. I should take this for a jest, if it did not regard matrimony. But however you may decorate your marriage-edifices with conversational gargoyles, your main purpose in their building is serious, I know.

MRS. HILLER. Thank you, love. You understand me.

MISS BLACK. I wish I could return the compliment.

MRS. HILLER. I couldn't jest more seriously. I am like the variegated philosophers who made Wisdom dance to their cap-and-bells, and observe the beats of their bauble. If you won't have my *protégé* for love of *him,* have him for love of me.

MISS BLACK. Then you are mad, quite mad. For what terrible crime, my poor Annette, has Heaven escheated your birthright of feminine instinct? Why, you might be a man! A man couldn't have trodden more clumsily on the delicate trimmings of a woman's mind.

MRS. HILLER [*aside*]. Oh, grant me patience! The delicate trimmings of Edith's mind!

MISS BLACK. You try to put upon me another woman's leavings, a lover who loves me and loves me not; and all this you blurt over me like a baby whose feeding-bottle is suddenly withdrawn.

MRS. HILLER. Another woman's leavings? Not in your sense. Clara would have had him if she would have had anyone. She said so. But she is not for marriage. She is for religion—a Sisterhood, or something of the kind: she was always Ritualist, you know, and keeps a Director.

MISS BLACK. Director? she has a board of Directors, as if her soul were a mining-concern, and is so public with her spiritual affairs that half Aldham may be said to have shares in it: yet it is the worst-managed soul in the world, for it cannot declare dividends enough of charity to reimburse its involuntary shareholders for the attention they have been obliged to sink in it.

MRS. HILLER. Your anger is vanished with her character. That is much more pleasant. But I can tell you further—Laura Brown would take him quickly enough if I didn't watch him from her.

MISS BLACK. Laura Brown? Then he has a fortune?

MRS. HILLER. You do justice to Laura. A competence now, a fortune hereafter. He is heir to a Staffordshire estate, the holder of which is an octogenarian uncle. I know it from my cousin, who lives near the place. How Laura learned it, I can't guess.

MISS BLACK. That Laura wants him is the one real argument you have brought forward, Annette. If I weren't engaged, it would be irresistibly tempting to take him out of Laura's hands.

MRS. HILLER [*aside*]. I thought so. She loves Laura more than words could express—unless they were *very* bad ones. [*Aloud.*] I knew that once you came to laugh at my proposal you would appreciate it.

MISS BLACK. It's so ridiculously original that it's hard to be seriously angry with you.

MRS. HILLER. I flatter myself it *is* original. Now you take it in a proper spirit, love. You see that these are things to laugh and be sensible about. It is a foolish tradition which makes us take this boy Eros and his baby-bites so seriously. If he bites too hard, you shake him and set him off your knee. Now, you'll go home, and think about this. And by the time Mr. Mortimer comes to you, you'll treat him kindly.

MISS BLACK. You're not going to carry this joke further, you wild creature?

MRS. HILLER. No, *you* must do that. Get away; Mr. Mortimer will be here directly. I'll send him to you as soon as I've finished with him.

MISS BLACK. If you do anything of the kind, I'll not only reject him, but snub him—not on his account, poor fellow, but as the only way of making *you* feel it. Now, Annette, I'm serious.

MRS. HILLER. With that face? Play out the play, dearest; don't spoil the last act, when I've had such trouble to bring it about. I see little of your boasted friendship. If I had interfered in the serious affairs of life—if I had asked you to defy the fashion, or change your milliner; but when I only ask you to change a husband—! I don't say, "Dress to please me"; I say only, "Marry to please me":

And you are so strait,
And so ingrateful, you deny me this!

MISS BLACK. Mad, mad, mad!—Well, I don't want to meet him here and now; but if you do—! [*Exit.*]

MRS. HILLER [*solus*]. Go, go, you sand-spout in petticoats! I might be a man, might I?—Madcap ways with madcap girls. I've stamped young Mortimer into your mind better than a conventional fashion could have done it. And there is more in my calculations than is dreamed of in your surmises. For now will she go home and find John Cumberland's letter—it must be there by this time—and then what she calls my heartless counsels will begin to prick into her mind; like an ear of wild barley thrust up your sleeve, which you laugh at for some two hours, and never laugh at again for the rest of your life. I'm sure he said he wrote to her by the same post as to me; so his letter must have reached her now, if it did not before she left home. Let me read his letter again, though. I'm sure, but I would be safe. [*Searching in a drawer.*] Oh, here it is. If he talked as he writes, Edith and he would have been too evenly matched to talk at at all. From the equality of opposing forces comes equilibrium, and from the equipoise of rival loquacities must come (I take it) silence. [*Reads.*] "I will have no more to do with your sex till either my head is stronger, or my heart less strong. I have tried wine and women—that dear hackneyed alliteration—and find that I can touch neither yet keep my brain. The illusions of the youth are infinite. He looks on a globe of grapes, and says—'Behold the golden ore of joy!' he looks on a group of girls, and says—'What an unworked mine of love!' He does not know that the one is only a cluster of headaches, and the other a cluster of heartaches. Or he thinks that he may taste the mere amity of a girl without heartache, as he might the mere juice of the grape without headache. That is what I have done; the more fool I! You may stop at the must of wine, at the must of love you will hardly stop. A girl's friendship is unfermented love; and you never awake to the settings-in of fermentation, till you find the fate of Noah. I am feeling shamefully like Noah. You will say our sex prepares the ferment. That's true: it is the excellent foolery of man that he rests content with nothing innocent till he has perverted it to his hurt; he is the devirginator of Nature, he cannot have to do with grapes and barley without debauching them. Into what of Nature the Curse could not turn venomous, man instils his toxic self, and is stung by retorted venom from his own veins; being himself, indeed, the authentic Curse, and the poison wherewith Earth is poisoned. Yet, now I think on it, we but return our wrongs on your sex; for the tooth which bit the Apple was the primal poison-fang—yes, Eve's tooth had death in it before the adder's. Which all is prologue to the fact, that I proposed the other day to Edith Black, in a sudden access of youth to the brain; and, being sobered, I have written to her by this post, asking release. You may think it unmanly, or think it manly, as you please. But stand my friend so far as to soften it to her. Tell her that if by my present proceeding I give her heartache, my own aches to give it her; and it is done to spare us both worse heartache in the future."

My dear boy, her pride will ache a good deal more than her heart.—"Stand my friend so far as to soften it to her."—Doesn't that reek of man like a stale smoking-compartment? They lay all their troubles to our causing, but—*"cherchez la femme?"* Yes; the first thing a man does when he gets into a scrape, is to come to some woman to get him out of it. And when a man has anything particularly unpleasant to face, he runs away and leaves some woman to face it for him. No, you selfish creature; I'll send young Mortimer to soften it to her. And don't weep about Edith's aching heart: her heart is not of a valetudinarian constitution, Heaven be praised! Mr. Cumberland, I thank you for your collaboration in my strategy. You didn't mean it, but I am generous—I thank you. No-one can call me heartless over this. This is not my doing. This is a special interposition of Providence, which is always on the side of the great generals. Someone has said something like that before;—aye, it was the little Corsican with the cancer in his stomach, I think: it is with genius as with blood, succession will out.—*Am* I heartless, I wonder? No, I think not. It's not heartless to interfere with the Loves of the Butterflies.—Mr. James?—No; he never had a chance, and she would have made him miserable had he got her. I wouldn't knowingly interfere with *him*. It would be as difficult for a woman to handle him without hurting him, as to fix a pastel with spray and not damage it. Not that I like him: he's an uncomfortable, distant youth, and I think he carries Gehenna in his breast-pocket; but he's no butterfly, and I respect him, though I'm the last person he'd suspect of it. Now *my* butterfly is a pretty butterfly, and will match her prettily. And I'm fond of him, or I wouldn't have done so much for him. I suppose I'm at the age when women take an interest in pretty boys. I wouldn't marry him myself, but it's very interesting to marry him to someone else. The worst of it is, my butterfly's been fluttering round three girls, and the one he likes best is neither Clara nor Edith, but Laura Brown. That's a picture in his heart to which I didn't direct Edith's attention. Now, in the first place, Laura would spoil his life—therefore he oughtn't to marry her. In the second place I hate Laura—therefore he shan't marry her. And if she gets to know of his prospects she'll snap him like a pike—little mercenary cat—so I must precipitate matters. [*Enter* SERVANT.]

SERVANT. Miss Brown, ma'am. [*Exit.*]

MRS. HILLER. Oh, that wretched girl! How *shall* I get rid of her? If he comes—and if they leave together—and if he should propose to the wrong one before I have a chance—— [*Enter* MISS BROWN.]

MRS. HILLER. Dear Laura, how *do* you do? So glad to see you, *etc.* [*Chat, chat, chat. Presently:—*]

MISS BROWN. Oh, do you know? Mr. Mortimer proposed to me last night.

MRS. HILLER. You don't say so! And you—?

MISS BROWN. Oh, of *course!*

MRS. HILLER. Of course. It's what one would naturally expect. [*Aside.*] But may I fall upon my own hat-pin if I am sure *what* is "of course!"

MISS BROWN. Very nice, but not at *all* the kind of man, you know——

MRS. HILLER. Oh, not at *all!* I *quite* agree with you. [*Aside.*] Oh, Providence is certainly on my side!

MISS BROWN. We've neither of us any nonsense on this subject, Annette; we think alike, I know: and for a girl who aspires to an ambitious marriage——

MRS. HILLER [*aside*]. I'll knead her into my scheme as a weevil is kneaded into bread. [*Aloud.*] That is just what I don't understand, Laura. In other respects I can quite comprehend he is not the kind of man you would fancy: but surely the heir to an estate in Staffordshire, with only an old uncle between him and it——

MISS BROWN. What is this!

MRS. HILLER. Do you mean to say you knew nothing of it?

MISS BROWN. Not a word! Oh, Annette! And you knew this all the time, and never told me! I take it of you most unkindly, Annette.

MRS. HILLER. How should I have guessed you didn't know it? He never made any secret of it with me, so I never dreamed he did with others. I supposed it was a matter of general knowledge. And we never happened to talk on the subject. My poor dear!

MISS BROWN. To think, to think—oh, Annette!

MRS. HILLER [*aside*]. I have fairly astonished you into candour! [*Aloud.*] My love, it's not irreparable. He'll make two bites at such a very charming cherry, or you're not the clever girl I take you for. He'll come back. The burnt child doesn't always dread the fire.

MISS BROWN. That's true. Without vanity, I don't think it will take much, as you say—— [*Smiling.*]

MRS. HILLER. Ah, you're better off than poor Edith! That reminds me, Laura, *would* you call upon our friend Edith on your way home? I fear she has had a great disappointment, and no-one can console her so well as you, who were her school-companion.

MISS BROWN. Indeed? How? I never heard of it. *Do* tell me!

MRS. HILLER. Did you never hear of her engagement to Mr. Cumberland?

MISS BROWN. To Mr. Cumberland? No, never!

MRS. HILLER. Ah, well, I'm not certain of it; it's all report, very likely.

But still, I *have* heard——. And I have heard that it has been broken off on his part, most *shamefully* for her, poor girl!

MISS BROWN. Poor girl! No, I never heard.

MRS. HILLER. And what makes it worse for her; I believe she only accepted him because she knew Mr. Mortimer was in love with you, and never dreamed you wouldn't take him. Keep that to yourself. If she knew what you have told me of last night, it might be the best consolation you could offer her.

MISS BROWN [*aside*]. She shan't have it, if this woman will hold her tongue! [*Aloud.*] I'll go now. Any consolation I can give poor Edith in such a trial——

MRS. HILLER. Mind, it's perhaps only report. So you mustn't mention *my* name——

MISS BROWN. No, of course. Not on any account!

MRS. HILLER. You must be very careful to insinuate it as mere rumour. Gently and *tactfully,* you know.

MISS BROWN. Oh! quite so. You may trust it to me. Poor Edith! Well, well! Good-bye, then, Annette.

MRS. HILLER. Good-bye.

MISS BROWN. By the way, Annette. About that other consolation.

MRS. HILLER. Yes?

MISS BROWN. She needn't know.

MRS. HILLER. Very well, little shrewdness! She shan't. Good-bye. [*Exit* MISS BROWN. MRS. HILLER *takes three waltz-steps.*]

MRS. HILLER [*solus*]. Providence *is* on the side of the great generals! First of all, what would have utterly ruined my plans is frustrated, completely frustrated, by this benignant Providence. Then, by an inspiration, I am enabled to converge upon Edith, at the decisive moment, the man who has discarded her and the woman who has rejected Willie Mortimer. For now that girl will go and *console* Edith! console her!—Oh, *how* she will console her! And if my pretty boy comes up while Edith is reeling between these alternate strokes, and does not utterly bungle his assault—the Lord hath delivered her into our hands! And Laura—Annette, admire your own subtlety!—Laura won't tell her that she has rejected young Mortimer—I have secured that, by making Laura think that Edith would be glad to have him: for Laura has manifestly repented, and wants him for herself. Yet she has gone blindly to aid in marrying him to her rival! It is a beautiful combination. Alas, that such strategic masterpieces can never be shown to one sympathising friend! Oh, the pity of it! My unknown genius must rest content with its solitary self-approbation. It is the lot of all genius above the vulgar herd. Well, Annette, your self-approbation is great, that is one comfort. [*Enter* SERVANT.]

SERVANT. Mr. Mortimer, ma'am. [*Exit.*]

MRS. HILLER. Now for the last manoeuvre. It ought not to be the most difficult. [*Enter* MR. MORTIMER.]

MRS. HILLER. Dear Mr. Mortimer, I am so glad to see you. Sit down.

MR. MORTIMER. You wanted to see me, I think?

MRS. HILLER. Yes, I did. Yet—yet I hardly know how to begin. It is very difficult, I find.

MR. MORTIMER. Dear Mrs. Hiller,——

MRS. HILLER. Yes, yes, I know what you would say. Between such attached friends as ourselves—yet it is a difficult matter to speak about. Nothing but openness and straightforwardness will serve my turn with you, I know; and those are not generally considered feminine weapons, are they? [*With a little laugh.*] If it were not that I feel your honour is at stake, no less than poor Edith's happiness——

MR. MORTIMER. My—my honour? Ed—do you mean Miss Black?

MRS. HILLER. I do. Dear Mr. Mortimer, what are your intentions with regard to Miss Black?

MR. MORTIMER. My in—— my intentions?

MRS. HILLER. Oh, now I have been too abrupt, and have offended you, I fear. Believe me, only necessity——. It is necessary to deal plainly with you, even if I give some pain, most unfortunate and unwilling pain, to your delicate feelings.

MR. MORTIMER. My intentions?

MRS. HILLER. Yes. I hope they are serious; for it is my duty to tell you that you have gone too far with her for any honourable retreat. I fear, oh, I very much fear, too far for Edith's happiness.

MR. MORTIMER. Oh—a—I say, Mrs. Hiller!

MRS. HILLER. No? do not tell me that my worst fears——

MR. MORTIMER. They—a—I fear they—they *are*.

MRS. HILLER. I cannot believe it! I cannot believe it!

MR. MORTIMER. Upon my honour, I never dreamed of this. This—oh, this is dreadful for a fellow, you know, Mrs. Hiller!

MRS. HILLER. Dreadful for you, is it? Think what it is for *her*. Pardon me if, at this moment, I cannot think even of *your* feelings, when I think what I believe—nay, what I know——. We were friends, you see. Oh, my poor Edith!

MR. MORTIMER. It—it's a deuce of a scrape. I beg your pardon. But what do you expect me to do?

MRS. HILLER. Nothing but what your own feelings prompt. The feelings of a gentleman should be a better guide than I in such a matter.

MR. MORTIMER. You think I should—in fact, a—propose to her?

MRS. HILLER. I can only repeat my former answer.

MR. MORTIMER. But—oh! this is a deu—— I beg your pardon. But you see, Mrs. Hiller, the fact is I—I—proposed to Miss Brown last night.

MRS. HILLER. Oh, I am sorry to hear this! I am very sorry to hear this!

MR. MORTIMER. And she—a—rejected me.

MRS. HILLER. Rejected you? And you could throw away your heart, your heart as *I* know it, upon a girl who does not value it; when it was in honour owed to a girl like Edith? I could not have thought it!

MR. MORTIMER. It's a fact, though.

MRS. HILLER. Well, if, to say truth, I thought your duty clear before, this makes it something more than clear; imperative, nay instant. Too surely Miss Brown will see Edith—perhaps before the day is over. And if Edith once learns what you have done, pride will force her to refuse what her heart aches to accept.

MR. MORTIMER. Do you mean——

MRS. HILLER. I mean that if you are going to carry out the intention you expressed, you should not linger here, but go at once, and forestall Miss Brown.

MR. MORTIMER [*aside*]. I didn't remember I'd expressed any intention! But I'm so dreadfully confused.

MRS. HILLER. That is the only way to save the poor girl from her own pride. Ah! you don't know women's hearts, Mr. Mortimer!

MR. MORTIMER. A—it seems I don't. I had no idea my attentions——

MRS. HILLER. Oh, your modesty, Mr. Mortimer, prevents you from placing the value on your attentions which others must needs do. You will take my advice, then, and go straight from here, without losing time where a girl's lifelong happiness may depend on your promptitude? It is noble, it is like you!

MR. MORTIMER. I will—yes, I will. No lady shall be a sufferer through my stupidity.

MRS. HILLER. It is like you, I can say no more. And perhaps you will find that your attentions, after all, were a truer index to your secret feelings than yourself quite knew.

MR. MORTIMER. Miss Black is a nice girl, I won't deny: I always liked her, though I did not think——

MRS. HILLER. I said, just now, you did not know a woman's heart. Ah, perhaps, Mr. Mortimer, you did not know your own. Good-bye. This restores the opinion of you in which I had weakly wavered.

MR. MORTIMER. It is consoling——

MRS. HILLER. Yes, it is *very* consoling to find that you are as I had always believed you. Good-bye, dear Mr. Mortimer. [*Exit* MORTIMER.]

MRS. HILLER [*going to window*]. O Sun of Austerlitz! If this were not England, where the sun travels *incognito,* there you *must* be!

## SCENE II

Miss Black's drawing-room. MR. MORTIMER *discovered. He has paid a flying-visit to his house on the way, and contrived to complete a toilette for the occasion.*

HE. She will be with me as soon as she is disengaged. Now, who the deuce can she have with her? [*Puts his hat on a chair, and drops his gloves on the floor.*] Seems to me, the more I think of it, that I've been a fool. Why the devil did I let that woman send me here? How has it all happened? Hanged if I can understand. Well, here I am, and I'm in for it now and no mistake. Why has one anything to do with women? From the moment you traffic with them, you never know either their intentions or your own. From nothing a woman says to you or does with you can you be sure you know what she's at. She's as many meanings as a Chinese word, and it's as hard for a poor foreign devil to get the trick of her: she's like the concentric advertisements, which you can box the compass and read from every point of it; but she doesn't read the same all round—no, there's the difference; she's a meaning for every point of the radius, and not two alike; oh, she can blow in a vicious circle like a Spring wind, and from as many quarters at once! But is it possible to comprehend beings whose mental anatomy is infinitely more remote from ours than the bodily one? Conceive a thing that can riot for an hour—an hour —in the dizzy delights of turning out its drawer? Oh, they do it—I've seen 'em. They say—"What shall we do? We've read the last novel, and the new number of the *Bread-and-Milk Magazine* hasn't come: let's go up stairs and turn out our drawers." And to see the things that come out of those drawers! Useless ends of ribbon neatly folded; little boxes, with little things in 'em that must have been devised to frame a colourable excuse for the existence of the box; a wild collection which harmonises only in the one point that everything belonging to it is equally trivial and equally useless: and each with a little history attached more trivial than the object it's attached to. There's the enthralment; to retail to each other those histories, and be astonished to find—like Diogenes with a difference—how many things they have which they don't want. It fills a man with an insatiable longing to turn out their brains, and see if the contents match those of their drawers. Only—only there wouldn't be enough brain to occupy him for an hour. But, hang it! they've brains enough to send me here against my will, and keep me here against my will, and make me propose to a girl against my will, and marry her against my will. The difference can't be in our brains, it must be in the uses we put 'em to.—Wish she would come. What an age she is! [*It is exactly a minute since he entered the room.*] How *do* you begin, I wonder? Wish I'd had time to ask some fellow how *he* began. Last night's no precedent; that was an impromptu, and a confoundedly bad one. Some fellows, I think, go down on one knee. Ought it to be one knee or both knees? One knee or both knees, that is the——. Suppose I go down on one knee as she comes in, and say——. No; I'm sure I couldn't do it. Really, I couldn't do it, you know! [*With an expostulating glance at the mantelpiece.*] I should feel—I should feel—as if she were a Bishop!

VOICE FROM THE PARLOUR. And so, dear,——

HE. Who's that?—It's that Brown girl! What is *she* doing here? If—if she's telling her about last night! [*Sits down overcome.*] I wish I had never come here! Couldn't I get away now? No; I must see the thing through: Mrs. Hiller would never let me hear the end of it. The end of it?—I haven't seen the beginning yet! Come, come; it needn't be about that they're talking. I shall soon be able to tell when she comes into the room. And Mrs. Hiller would certainly call it cowardice if I went now,—there is such an unreasoning prejudice in the human mind against running away! Yet flight is a subtly daring form of courage—I reasoned it out for my British comfort after Majuba Hill. To turn your back on a man is the supremest expression of contempt. Then you best exhibit your defiance by turning your back upon the foe, heroically insult him to his face by showing him the reverse of yours, and scorn him to his very teeth by running from him worse than death. There's precedent for it, moral and historical. The Puritan wing at Marston Moor, when Rupert charged it, won the battle by the headlong valour with which it ran away. It is by flight that Christians overthrow the devil—rout his forces, horse and foot, by stubborn giving way before 'em. To see how retrograde valour is scandalled among the unthinking of this world. There's proof casuistic for the thesis, too. According to all sound casuists, oaths made under compulsion are null and of no force, —why, the same then with taking to your heels: if you take to your heels under compulsion, your flight is null and invalid; the more compulsion, the more invalid; the more panic, therefore, the more void your flight, and the harder running you do, the clearer it is you have done none. Oh, it is plain as a pike-staff; if I fled from here, I could convince myself of courage before all the schools in Europe—but alas! Mrs. Hiller hasn't been through the schools. Reason is thrown away on a woman. There's another method: I notice that when people please to commit a baseness, but don't please to have it thought so, they say they do it in accordance with their principles, call it by some name with the adjective "higher" before it, and baseness is nobility. A man comes to you, for instance, and tells you, you are selfish. You explain that you are merely acting in accordance with your principles, and that what *he* took for selfishness is in reality the Higher Egoism. He is rebuked, and goes away confounded at having attacked anything so magnificent as the Higher Egoism. Oh, it works all round! You find continency troublesome, you practice the Higher Purity, which the gross might unhappily mistake for the lower sensuality; you find originality troublesome, you practice the Higher Plagiarism. Ah! it is the wittiest fashion since Parliament took up arms against the King for the King's protection, rebelled against him in his own name, and that his head might not be turned by evil counsellors, took it off! I look every day to find some burglar explaining that he breaks into houses at the imperious dictates of his conscience, being a follower of the Higher Burglary. And why may not I, finding boldness troublesome, practice the Higher Courage; and explain to Mrs. Hiller that I am following my principles in the teeth of an uncomprehending world? Why, because I haven't firmness enough to run away,

> "Oh, when will this long, weary—call—have end,
> And lend me leave to come unto my——"

no; I mean lend her leave to come to me. Singular, how full I am of trains of nonsense, and scraps of verse! One would say I was light-headed. Very singular; I haven't read Spenser since I was a boy, and head of the school in verse. Why should I remember him now? They say it *is* that way with men that are—but then I'm *not* in love, there's the deuce of it!

VOICE OF MISS BROWN. And he said—— [*A burst of laughter.*]

HE. Oh, good God! She *is* telling her! [*A frightful interregnum of cold perspiration.*] It's just what I remember one of those old dramatists says. One of those fellows like the Greek comic dramatists, that no decent people read, but only British Museum people, and poets, and clergy of the Universities qualifying for a Bishopric.* He says, once you lodge your heart with women, you have a more whimsical lodging than a fellow that lives in a windmill. He mayn't have been a decent fellow, but he knew what he was talking about there, by Jove! I'm a puppet in the hands of destiny, or I should never be so turned about by this sixteenth-hand kind of amorousness, this *simulacrum* of sexual attraction, wavering hither and thither. Pervasive Ibsen! *magnus est Ibsen et prevalebit.* I guess the Norwegian fellow's right; it's heredity, and some beast of an ancestor is using me for his own selfish purposes. There's metempsychosis in loves, not a doubt of it. Love is a

* Mortimer is *not* a University-man, and his ideas on the Universities are something musty.

wassail-candle, set in successive bodies like successive sconces, till it gutters feebly out in the odd twentieth. My loves were loved and staled by the improvident fellows before me, who never took a thought of *me,* never considered it was *my* love they were running through, *my* erotic portion they were gaming away at the table of life. This is a superannuated emotion quartered on my luckless body, like an ancient dependant, by some testating progenitor; the remainder-passion of some Pyrrhonic gallant who could never make up his mind whether in the grammar of love there were any degrees of comparison.—If I were any kind of a man at all, my chance would be less desperate, perhaps, even now. If I could *do* anything, if I had ever made a figure in anything! If I had been a politician,—she admires Gladstone, I know, because he once wrote a post-card to her brother's friend's friend, who had heard Gladstone explain something, and wrote to ask him to explain the explanation. No-one could explain the explanation of the explanation when it came; but no matter—she admires him. It was like the manna, it savoured to each one what he would have it; and would you desire a better ha'p'orth of exposition? Now, if I perorated at public meetings in the pretty, popular meteorological style:—"The veteran statesman's sunlike career is drawing to its glorious close," *et cetera.* "Sunlike career"—why, so it is; for like the sun, he has declined from his Blue firmament and sets in Red. Odd's my life! (as they say in Elizabethan plays): your sun is your only breeder of metaphors; he breeds them out of your poet like flies out of carrion. You lay your poet out in a hot July day, and he is soon a corrupt mass of imagery; he crawls with similitudes, and taints the neighbourhood with ill-smelling fancy. Your husbandman could sooner do without the sun than your poet. If there were no other reason but his poverty of sun, one would know an Esquimau singer must have poverty of wit; it passes the fantasy of men to conceive a hyperborean Muse. In the Arctic circles the Muses must hibernate like celestial dormice. Until a bountiful Providence make the poet's brain as sustenant as the bear's paw, he can never suck it through the Polar nights.—I'll forswear that rascal James; I did but talk with him last evening, and I had such a surfeit of Elizabethan that it's rising on my stomach at intervals like a sour eructation. Ah, if I were like him, now! a scribbling fellow—what the newspapers call "a brilliant young writer of the rising school." By Jove! one of the new sect in literature that he talks about, founded by an Edinburgh Editor. He is a literary Tolstoi, James says, who has shared all his mental estate amongst the young men his followers: and they practice a manner of intellectual Socialism, a Voluntary Poverty of ideas; for personal property in views is forbidden among 'em, they throw all their wits into a community-purse, and when any one of them needs an opinion, he takes it out of the common stock. Guess that would work well for a fellow like me, who put in a pennyworth of his own notions, and took out a pound's-worth of others!—I think I hear them coming out! It's too late for the Higher Courage. I'll go through with it: I always went through with things, and I'll go through with this. But I'll never go through with another, hang me if I do! [*Voices emerge into the passage.*]

HE. It's all over. She's coming. My God! can they hear my heart in the street, I wonder?

VOICE OF MISS BROWN. Then if I hear any more talk, I can say there is no foundation?

VOICE OF MISS BLACK. None whatever.

VOICE OF MISS BROWN. I'm so glad—for your sake, dearest. I thought it couldn't be—— [*Voices recede towards the door.*]

HE. *Has* she told her? [*Enter* MISS BLACK.]

SHE [*aside*]. He's here! Surprising woman! I'll have him, if it's only to spite that wretch, Jack, and that worse wretch, Laura. [*Aloud and cordially.*] *So* sorry to have kept you waiting.

HE. Oh—a—don't mention it! I've been very comfortable.

SHE [*aside*]. Doesn't look it. Yes, he's dressed himself for the part, I see.

HE. I've called to see you. [*Aside.*] I couldn't have said anything more foolish if I'd tried!

SHE. It is so kind of you. I was just saying to Laura how long it was since you'd called: but no hints will make that girl go before she's said her last word of chatter.

HE [*aside*]. She's not told her! [*Wipes his face in the sudden revulsion of relief.*]

SHE [*sympathetically*]. You are hot, Mr. Mortimer?

HE. Oh, no, thank you; quite cool.

SHE [*aside*]. A Naiad couldn't look cooler! Poor fellow!

HE [*aside*]. I begin to realise it *isn't* all over. Would it were! [*Aloud.*] I—I called because I wanted to see you—very particularly, Miss Black.

SHE [*softly, looking suddenly out of the window*]. Yes!

HE [*aside*]. I wish she wouldn't look away from me like that! [*Aloud.*] I've just come from Mrs. Hiller's.

SHE [*aside*]. Surely, he's not going to *tell* me that she made him come!

HE. And—and——

SHE [*more softly, looking at him*]. Yes, dear Mr. Mortimer?

HE [*aside*]. It's no use, I never shall if she looks at me like that! [*Aloud.*] And—what a charming woman she is, Miss Black!

SHE [*aside*]. *Did* he come here to tell me that another woman is charming?

HE. Very sincere, don't you think?

SHE [*aside*]. What in mercy have I to do with Annette's sincerity? And *now!* [*Aloud.*] Oh, I hope not, Mr. Mortimer!

HE. A—surely you think sincerity one of the divinest qualities in woman? You, for instance, could not be insincere.

SHE. Oh, it may be divine, Mr. Mortimer, but it isn't human. Insincerity is one of the qualities which distinguish us from the beasts. Don't think me deficient in the attributes of the higher animals. [*He smiles feebly, and seems to feel the jest excruciatingly mistimed.*]

SHE [*aside*]. Oh, my tongue, my tongue! What a time to choose a mock sentiment! But *why* will he be so provoking? [*Aloud.*] Don't think me frivolous. Indeed, I feel the reverse of frivolous.

HE. Oh, not at all! [*Relapses into dead silence.*]

SHE [*aside*]. Provoking man! There's nothing for it, I see, but to let the conversation drift, and watch my chance to give *him* a chance. So I must settle down patiently to talk. [*Aloud.*] What places have you been to since I last saw you, Mr. Mortimer?

HE [*brightening with exasperatingly manifest relief*]. Oh,—a—lots of places. I was at the Mantons' last night. Mr. Bailey was there —do you know him?

SHE. I have met him once. As he is one of the few cultivated men in Alcester, I can't well forget the fact.

HE. Collects pictures, you know, corresponds with Ruskin, and writes a little—unsuccessfully.

SHE. I know. But didn't you find him rather a bore, like all these people with a mania, who will talk about nothing else? More Rossettian than Rossetti, and Pre-Raphaelitish while the rest of the world has moved on? Nothing antique will pass with him later than Perugino, at the furthest; and nothing modern which is not antique. He'll be vastly disappointed with Heaven, unless the Almighty has designed his angels in the manner of Burne-Jones; and will expect to find the walls of Paradise frescoed by the spirit of Botticelli.

HE. Ha, ha! a little that way. We asked him about his writing, but he made light of it. "I've cast much manuscript on the editorial waters," he said; "and Scripture was justified in it, for I found it again after many days—on my breakfast-table."

SHE. Did the company take him?

HE. Not many, I think. You know Mrs. Smith? Well, she said: "Dear Mr. Bailey, what is an editor like? I never saw a real editor."

SHE. Just what she *would* say!

HE. "An editor," says he, "from the point of view of the young contributor, is an automatic machine, into which you drop a manuscript and a guinea appears." Fletcher was there, you know; I suppose Mrs. Smith wasn't aware he was an editor. He said: "An editor is unlike any other automatic machine, for he always works." I fancy some editors manage to do precious little in that line, though.

SHE [*aside*]. Annette was right; he isn't a fool. I never really took the trouble to investigate him before.

HE. Then some one started a discussion on the appropriate excellencies of husbands and wives—there were plenty of 'em at table—and you might have fancied yourself at a dinner of letter-writers to the *Daily Telegraph,* listening to *Paterfamilias,* and *A British Wive,* and *One Who has Tried,* in the flesh.

SHE. Every girl—and man too, I dare say—has dear ideas on that subject. I confess to some. Will you acknowledge the weakness?

HE. Why—a—a little.

SHE. I'll give you the catalogue of my potential perfections, if you'll give me yours. Is it a bargain?

HE. Done.

SHE. Oh, I should be a model British wife, I promise you! Well, *imprimis,* I would sew buttons on my husband's shirts whenever he particularly wanted to put them on, and said—"Oh, that'll do; I'd sooner go without a button than be kept waiting all this time!" Not before, on any account,—I know what is proper to a wife, I hope!

HE. A very fair beginning. You promise well, I see.

SHE. I'd leave my husband every freedom. He should go wherever he liked—to take me; if he were profanely given—not more than becomes a man of taste—he should swear *in camera,* and I would sort and lay out his oaths for him with his collars—little, perfumed, elegant trifles, related to the more fearful article as a saloon-pistol to a Derringer:—"by Jove"—I should have to look twice at "by Jove" [MORTIMER *looks guiltily conscious*]. If he were a hardened smoker he should smoke—cigarettes, as ladylike as money could buy them; he should have all his bachelor-friends, and I the criticism of them,——

HE. He wouldn't have them long, then.

SHE [*innocently*]. Would that be my fault, Mr. Mortimer? But there! now you've thrown me out; and you'll never know the roll of my wifely virtues till you ask it of my epitaph. Come, it's your turn; and I'll promise not to interrupt *you.*

HE. You must help me to set my ideas in order, then.

SHE. Well, of course; to begin with, you will let your wife have her way? That's indispensable.

HE. Certainly, for my wife's way would be my way.

SHE. You have shut two meanings in one sentence. Which am I to take?

HE. Whichever pleases you.

SHE. Or whichever would please your wife?

HE. It may be all the same, if you like.

SHE. The same—if I like? [*Aside.*] Now!

HE. Miss Black, I came here to-day——

SHE. Yes!

HE. To say—— [*Aside.*] It's no use; when she drops her eyes like that, I'm done! [*Aloud.*] What was I going to say? I forget.

SHE. Oh, don't trouble! I'm infinitely obliged to you!

HE. For what?

SHE. For your forbearing memory.

HE. For my forbearing memory?

SHE. I am thanking you that at the eleventh hour relenting thoughts have prevailed with you.

HE. What do you mean?

SHE. Oh, Mr. Mortimer, an epigram, like virtue, is its own reward; never be so superfluous as to demand a meaning! [*Aside.*] Neither lash nor coaxing can bring him to the leap. I hate him!

HE [*aside*]. What does she mean? I only see she's angry. What have I done?—Oh, it's all up! I'd better go. [*Aloud.*] I think it's time I went, Miss Black.

SHE. My temper is not contradictious, Mr. Mortimer!

HE [*aside*]. No, but it's something worse! This is a timely revelation! Heavens, what an escape I've had! [*Aloud.*] I meant, Miss Black, that I've remembered it's my dinner-hour, and I shall scarcely have time to get home.

SHE. Your memory shows most in-and-out running—that's the correct elegance of phrase, I believe?

HE [*aside*]. Oh, this is too hot! [*Aloud.*] Good evening.

SHE. Good evening.

HE [*aside*]. That girl can touch a hand with as many *nuances* as she would a piano! There was as much wrath in that hand-shake as in a clenched fist. [*Turning at the door with a last effort.*] A—a—by the way. My sister—I mean—if you like, you know, to call on her, she's always glad to see you.

SHE. Is your sister in the habit of making you her messenger? Women seem to have differing experience of your memory.

HE. Oh, come, Miss Black! You'll allow me sense enough to carry a message, I hope?

SHE. Alas! Heaven has not made me its Grand Almoner, Mr. Mortimer!

HE [*aside, standing paralysed for some seconds*]. Why, she's a little spitfire! Thank Fortune for my irresolution! No more asking of wives for me. O beatific Parisian dream of Smithfield! if there were ever truth in thee, let us return to the customs of our ancestors. Henceforward I'll turn monk—or Turk, keep the cloister—or a harem, that's certain; but no more asking of wives! [*Aloud.*] Then good evening. [*Exit.*]

SHE [*solus*]. I could cry for anger! Yet if I had only held patience, only held patience with him, just at that moment,—it might have been different. But oh!—who *could* hold patience with *him?*

HE [*returning*]. A—excuse me, Miss Black. I've left my hat. [*Aside.*] Why! she's tears in her eyes!

SHE. Your hat?—Here it is, on the chair. [*Handing it with several extra degrees of chill, to compensate for conscious detection.*]

HE. Thank you. Good-bye. [*Aside.*] They're there still, for all her coldness. Frost and thaw together is most feminine meteorology; one could only find it in a woman's book, or looks. [*Aloud.*] Good-bye.

SHE. Good-bye.

HE [*not stirring*]. Good-bye.

SHE [*looks at him, suddenly softens, and smiles archly*]. Don't you think you may as well leave go my hand, Mr. Mortimer?

HE [*suddenly*]. May—may I keep it? *Altogether?*

. . .

SHE. Well, and how long are you going to love me?

HE. Is it necessary to issue a guarantee with my love?

SHE. Yea, nowadays, most necessary. You should warrant it, as they do watches, to go for a year, or a month, or at least a week; and engage, if your love fail in the stipulated conditions, to supply me with a new one *gratis*. Perhaps a week is too unconscionable an exaction: warrant it to wear over-night, provided it be treated with ordinary care, and wound up in a proper manner.

HE. A good thought! My love needs winding up without delay, I find.

SHE. How quickly it runs down! It is only a minute since I wound it up before. That does not augur well for lasting; or else your love is an American watch, which no-one can wind up at a single sitting—except it were an all-night sitting. And do you know—*what* time did you say your dinner was?—that *this* sitting has been held for an hour over your hat?

HE. I would sit on a hundred hats!——

SHE. Nay, wait; you can ruin yourself in hats afterwards—*my* hats, Sir!

. . .

SHE [*solus*]. I have made a discovery! Who'd have suspected it in a god?—Eros is a rank Socialist. He allows no distinction, among his followers, between man and man. Up to the point of proposal, Jack and this man were different as fire and water; but after—really, it was very much the same. He *is* good-looking, and quite *nice* once you have got him past his shyness. Perhaps—perhaps Annette was right, and I can be pretty happy with any decent good fellow. It's a very comfortable state of mind—not heroic, but comfortable. After all, the consuming passion that poets talk about must be by very much more heroic than pleasant. It *may* be happiness to pine and lie awake of nights: but—Eros! cheerfulness and sleep, if you please; or nothing do you get of me. And he really *is* a nice boy,—not Eros, but the other.

[*And* HE *remarks to himself, as he steps into the street, that—*] A fellow doesn't really *know* how much he is in love with a girl until he tries!

# NOTES ON NEW POEMS OF FRANCIS THOMPSON

## REFERENCES

In the following notes a brief description of the manuscripts is given, together with their location in the Boston College Collection. When a manuscript is in a notebook, the number of the notebook is given. The original numbers have been retained on those notebooks that had been numbered when acquired. All others have been given numbers preceded by the letters, "B.C."

A POETIC SEQUENCE: The poems and arrangement of this sequence are the poet's, addressed, as were the *Ad Amicam* sonnets, to his friend, Katie King. This short-lived friendship was terminated chiefly because Katie King's mother considered the poems too ardent for a friendship which could not lead to marriage.

I. ELIJAH: final draft, ink, unsigned. This sonnet—a close parallel with Sonnet I of the *Ad Amicam* sequence—commemorates the welcome advent of this new friendship.

II. WAITING: final draft, ink, unsigned. Here is the poet's entreaty for a repeated sign of friendship.

III. FORGOING: final draft, ink, unsigned. Using the same imagery that in Sonnet I of the *Ad Amicam* sequence reveals the solace of this new friendship's coming, the poet here utters his *Fiat* to the dread fulfillment of that friendship's passing.

IV. "SO NOW, GIVE O'ER": final draft, ink, unsigned. This is the poet's final, stark Amen to the *Fiat* of the preceding sonnet.

"THIS VESSEL MAN": rough draft, ink, unsigned, Notebook 15, pp. 3, 5.

THE SOLEMN VOICE: rough draft, pencil, unsigned. (Cf. note on *My Song's Young Virgin Date.*)

FALSE LOVE AND TRUE: rough draft, pencil, unsigned, Notebook 50, pp. 9–10.

"HER FEET ARE EARTH": rough draft, pencil, unsigned, Notebook B.C. 10, pp. 33–34.

"I LOVE AND HATE THEE": rough draft, pencil, unsigned, Notebook 30, p. 10.

"YOU, WHILE THE GALE YOUR LOCKS UNBINDS": rough draft, unsigned, Notebook 43-A, p. 1.

"AS MORNING EYES FROM SLEEP AWAKENING": rough draft, pencil, unsigned.

"WAKE NOT THE STILL SAD YEARS": rough draft, pencil, unsigned.

*Valete:* final copy, ink, signed. Though the Latin title is plural, the poem would seem to require the singular.

TO CECILIA: corrected copy, pencil, unsigned, Notebook B.C. 14, pp. 31–32. The subject of these verses is unidentified. In the opinion of one close to the poet, they are the result of "some slight and casual encounter."

*Nisi Dominus:* rough draft, pencil, unsigned, Notebook 14-A, pp. 57–58. Illustrative of perfect agreement between the two poets in matters spiritual and æsthetic, this poem may be read with the following passage from Patmore.

> *Dear Lord, for forty years I tried to raise in the wilderness a house for Thy abode. I painfully gathered bricks, and worked a bit of cornice here, and there a capital; but as I put it together all would suddenly fall, and still I gathered up material, though the more I gathered the greater seemed the chaos; but one day, why none could tell, except perhaps that I felt more despair than ever I had done before, I heard a winnowing of unseen wings, and lo, the bricks and stones all took their place.* (THE ROD, THE ROOT AND THE FLOWER.)

"THE PERFECT WOMAN": rough draft, pencil, unsigned. The notation "(To follow *'Domus Tua'*)" is the poet's, indicating that the poem refers to Alice Meynell.

TO A WIND: final copy, ink, unsigned, with the title, *To a Wind of the South,* of which the last part is deleted. Thompson originally included this poem in the *Ad Amicam* series, inspired by Katie King.

THE BRIDE OF GOD AND THEE: corrected copy, ink, unsigned. This theme, the essence of Patmore's *The Angel in the House* and many of his Odes, found literal fulfillment in the relationship between Wilfrid and Alice Meynell. On a printed copy of this poem is the following note in Meynell's handwriting: "Lines set up for *Dublin Review* but not published. (Sept. 1917.)"

*De Mortuis:* corrected copy, pencil, unsigned. The identity of the child whose death inspired these lines, has not been established.

FRAGMENT OF HELL: final copy, ink, unsigned, Notebook 46-B, pp. 26–27. The close similarity of address in this poem and in *To W.M.* would seem to identify the poet's "friends" as Wilfrid and Alice Meynell.

AN UNAMIABLE CHILD: final copy, ink, unsigned. There is strange poignancy in this poem when the tenor of Thompson's life is remembered.

"GO, BOOK, THOU SHALT BE HAPPIER": rough draft, pencil, unsigned. Although no external evidence has been found, this poem would seem, beyond doubt, to be addressed to Alice Meynell.

*Ecce Ancilla Domini:* final copy, ink, unsigned, Notebook of Early Poems, pp. 32–33. This poem is difficult to appreciate without some knowledge of the painting by Dante Gabriel Rossetti which inspired it. In the best Pre-Raphaelite tradition, it portrays Our Lady as a girlish figure in white, crouched on her pallet, "with pensive eyes that yet are not afraid" fixed upon a white lily in the outstretched hand of a tall, wingless angel with "gravely noble face," standing erect, robed in white. A white dove is seen floating into the room through a window open upon a blue sky, the bright sunlight of an Eastern morning streaming into the room. In added contrast with the predominant white are the soft blue of the bed curtains, the reddish hair of Our Lady and the deeper red of a conventional screen in the foreground. The painting hangs in the National Gallery of British Art, popularly called the Tate Gallery.

"A BITTER FRIEND": rough draft, pencil, unsigned. Because of the allusion to "your gentle years," this sonnet cannot have been addressed to Alice Meynell who was twelve years the poet's senior, but to Katie King who was many years younger than Thompson. An added reason for thinking that this sonnet and the one that follows are addressed to Katie King, is the fact that final drafts of both were in the notebook containing the *Ad Amicam* sequence addressed to her.

"ALACK! MY DEEP OFFENCE": rough draft, pencil, unsigned.

"WHAT HAVE I LEFT": rough draft, pencil, unsigned. Seemingly addressed to Katie King, the "topless praise" previously given to another, is the praise of Alice Meynell in the sequence, *Love in Dian's Lap.*

MY SONG'S YOUNG VIRGIN DATE: rough draft, pencil, unsigned. The literal agreement of sentiment in *The Solemn Voice* and in this sonnet—especially l. 5—with an entry in one of Thompson's notebooks, would seem to indicate beyond doubt that the subject in both poems is Alice Meynell. The note is quoted by Viola Meynell.

> *I yielded to the insistent commands of my conscience and uprooted my heart—as I supposed. Later, the renewed presence of the beloved lady renewed the love I thought deracinated. For a while I swung vacillant. . . . I thought I owed it to her whom I loved more than my love of her finally to unroot that love, to pluck away the last fibres*

*of it, that I might be beyond treachery to my resolved duty. And at this second effort I finished what the first had left incomplete. The intial agony had really been decisive, and to complete the process needed only resolution. But it left that lady still the first, the one veritable, full-orbed and apocalyptic love of my life.* (FRANCIS THOMPSON AND WILFRID MEYNELL, p. 124.)

ADVERSITY: final copy, ink, unsigned, Notebook of Early Poems, pp. 42–43. This sonnet seems to have been inspired by Alice Meynell during the period of poetic silence, the end of which Thompson celebrates in *To a Poet Breaking Silence.* Viola Meynell, recording how enthralled was Thompson by her mother's versatility of mind, quotes from a letter he wrote in which Mrs. Meynell is described as: "A mistress of poetry, an exquisite critic, who knows besides, music . . . and all kinds of multifarious things."

SAD SEMELE: final copy, ink, signed. The poet's adaptation of the myth of Semele is, for one reader at least, too elusive for comprehension.

"LOVE, THOU HAST SUFFERED": rough draft, pencil, unsigned, Notebook B.C. 9, pp. 28–30. This sonnet was written to precede *Love's Varlets,* a sonnet included in Thompson's *Collected Poems.*

*Une Fille de Joie:* corrected copy, ink, unsigned, Notebook of Early Poems, pp. 74–76. The starkness of this indictment of Victorian Pharisaism springs from the haunting memory of the nightmare time of Thompson's days in the streets of London, when he was befriended by the *fille de joie* to whom he pays such tender tribute in *Sister Songs.* (Cf. Pt. I, ll. 289–96.)

CHORIC SONG OF FAUNS: fair copy, ink, signed, a duplicate of lines from the third scene of Thompson's *Pastoral Play,* the original manuscript of which, lacking the first scene, is in the Boston College Collection.

"'BEAUTY IS TRUTH, TRUTH BEAUTY'": corrected copy, pencil, unsigned, Notebook B.C. 9, p. 4. A challenge to the half-truth of Keats' famous line in the *Ode on a Grecian Urn.*

"ALL THINGS ARE JOY": rough draft, pencil, unsigned, Notebook B.C. 31, pp. 22, 24.

"I SAT WITH NATURE": rough draft, pencil, unsigned, Notebook B.C. 17, p. 11.

GENESIS: final copy, ink, unsigned. The poet's favorite theme of life through death is gently treated here.

"SING, BIRD, SING": rough draft, pencil, unsigned, Notebook B.C. 21, pp. 128–33.

"LEARN OF THE MOUTH OF THE MOON": rough draft, pencil, unsigned, Notebook B.C. 18, p. 25.

PROPHETIC VERSE: rough draft, pencil, unsigned, Notebook B.C. 5, pp. 13–14.

*"Maria intra Limina Æstuant":* final copy, ink, unsigned. Praise of "the checks and stops" of law directive of life and art, is of the essence of Thompson's poetry, as it is of Patmore's (cf. *Legem Tuam Dilexi*) and of Alice Meynell's (cf. *The Laws of Verse*).

A FAITHLESS SWORD: rough draft, pencil, unsigned.

"HE CAME TO ME": rough draft, pencil, unsigned, Notebook 41, pp. 3–4.

MADONNA AND CHILD: rough draft, pencil, unsigned, Notebook 41, pp. 1–2. The happy blend of realism and reverent familiarity in these lines is peculiarly Thompsonian.

WEEP FOR HIM: rough draft, pencil, unsigned.

*Dormiam et Requiescam:* corrected copy, pencil, unsigned, Notebook 42, p. 3. The peace of which Thompson here sings, as always, is not the cessation of strife, but the peace of final victory in strife that is coterminal with life.

THE JOY OF LIFE AND DEATH: rough draft, pencil, unsigned, Notebook 43-A, p. 8.

PATMORE AND *New Poems:* rough draft, pencil, unsigned. The futility of having dedicated *New Poems* to his friend, dead before the volume appeared, is the chief theme of this lament.

LINES ON PATMORE'S DEATH, I, II, III: rough drafts in pencil, unsigned. Number II is from Notebook B.C. 9, pp. 32–33. In these verses there are familiar echoes of *A Captain of Song* and the passage descriptive of Patmore in the *Ode for the Diamond Jubilee of Queen Victoria.*

"GOD! IF THOU SITT'ST IN HEAVEN": rough draft, pencil, unsigned, Notebook B.C. 28, p. 4. The Isaian tenor of these lines savors more of Patmore than of Thompson.

ENGLAND, OLD AND NEW: rough draft, pencil, unsigned, Notebook 8, pp. 2–3. The revived enmities of England, old and new, give these lines a topical interest in our day as in Thompson's.

*Fuit:* final copy, ink, signed. The cowardice and venality of England in Thompson's day, contrasted with the heroic militancy of Crécy and

Trafalgar, is one the of poet's favorite themes, notably in *The Nineteenth Century, Peace,* and *To England,* an ode printed in the *Academy,* March 19, 1898, but not included in Thompson's *Collected Poems.* One wonders what Thompson—who witnessed merely the harvest of the sowing of the wind—might have written had he known the reaping of the whirlwind in two World Wars and the threat of a third.

*Victoria Regina, In Memoriam:* rough draft, pencil, unsigned, Notebook 122, pp. 2–5. There is irony in these lines, in this day of the gradual dissolution of Victoria's Empire.

THE SCHOOLMASTER FOR GOD: rough draft, pencil, unsigned. An abridged version, with many verbal variations and lacking stanzas 6 and 8 to 11, was printed in the *Irish Rosary,* April, 1913, and reprinted April, 1957. The first line in stanza 15 of that version, which does not appear in our manuscript, is here added in italics, for completion of sense, although it may be an interpolation. This poem is the only one, elsewhere printed, that is included in this volume—an exception made in response to several requests, because in this version there are variant readings and five stanzas not elsewhere published. The title given the poem by Thompson is: *Stolen Fruit of Eden Tree.* The following footnote, written most probably by Wilfrid Meynell, was printed with the poem in the *Irish Monthly.*

> *"The Schoolmaster for God" is a characteristic phrase of Francis Thompson's coining. He uses it of John Baptist de la Salle, in his little* Life *of the Founder of the Brothers of the Christian Schools. And doubtless that is what every schoolmaster with a vocation sets out to be—what every schoolmaster without a vocation finds himself forced to be—so certainly do all roads of knowledge lead to the Omniscient. Comforting himself thus, Francis Thompson in these verses (partly set down as an exercise in imitative metre and now published for the first time) revived the very phrase of his prose, not refusing the great title to Lucifer even.*

THE LILY MAIDEN: corrected copy, ink, unsigned, Notebook of Early Poems, pp. 39–40.

IN THE GARDEN: corrected copy, ink, unsigned, Notebook of Early Poems, pp. 22–25.

A BALLAD OF FAIR WEATHER: final copy, ink, unsigned, Notebook of Early Poems, pp. 46–50.

THE TRAIN: rough draft, pencil, unsigned, Notebook 8, p. 1. Everard Meynell quotes Thompson's landlady at Crawley as saying: "It's very nice for Mr. Thompson; he's got the trains at the back every half hour or more, when he's in his bedroom." But "the thunderous horror of the train," it seems, brought less joy to the poet than "the furrowed silence" of its passing.

HORACE'S ODE ON LYCE: rough draft, ink, unsigned, Notebook B.C. 15, pp. 7–9. This metrical translation is unusually successful in felicitous phrasing and fidelity to the original.

THE POET JESTER: rough draft, pencil, unsigned, Notebook 15, pp. 24–25. This is one of many scraps of verse and doggerel on Paul Kruger of Boer War fame, familiarly called "Oom" ("Uncle") by his followers. "Peter" probably refers to Joubert, a political opponent of Kruger and leader of the progressive Boer element. "John" would seem to be Steyn, Commandant General of forces opposed to Kruger.

THE LARGER HOPE: corrected copy, ink, unsigned.

"THE VOICE OF THE TURTLE IS HEARD IN OUR LAND": (*Canticle of Canticles,* II, 12.) A rough draft, ink and pencil, unsigned, Notebook 47-A, pp. 41, 43. Charles Waterton in *Wanderings in South America,* records a ride on the back of a cayman, and a ride on a sea turtle is described by Louis de Rougemont in his *Adventures, as Told by Himself*—tall stories, it would seem, in Thompson's opinion.

GOING TO SCHOOL: corrected copy, pencil, unsigned, Notebook 23-A, pp. 16–17. Interesting verses as thoughts of a boy who was "father of the man"—Thompson.

"I SHOWED TO ALL MY GOODLY FRUIT": corrected copy, pencil, unsigned. The poet of "Things as they are," is here contrasted with *No Singer of His Time.*

ON A REVIEWER, CALLING MY POETRY "AMBITIOUS": rough draft, pencil, unsigned, Notebook B.C. 9, pp. 22–24. Reviewing *New Poems* in the *Speaker* (June 5, 1897), Quiller-Couch wrote: "In some of the ambitious poems, ambitiousness is perilously near pretentiousness."

NO SINGER OF HIS TIME: corrected copy, pencil, unsigned, Notebook 33, pp. 9–10. Apropos the title and theme of this poem, it is interesting to recall G. K. Chesterton's words in *The Victorian Age in Literature.*

> *None of the Victorians were able to understand Francis Thompson; his sky-scraping humility, his mountains of mystical detail, his occasional and unashamed weakness, his sudden and sacred blasphemies. Perhaps the shortest definition of the Victorian Age is that he stood outside it.*

DEEPLY-SINNING MAN: rough draft, pencil, unsigned.

A PASSING SONG: final draft, ink, signed. The familiar theme of these verses—the greater beauty and depth of poetry that springs from suffering and death—is developed with greater success in such poems as *Laus Amara Doloris.*

"THE WATER TO THE STAR RETURNS": corrected copy, pencil, unsigned.

A FOOL BY NATURE AND BY ART: rough draft, pencil, unsigned, Notebook B.C. 9, p. 13. A fragment.

"O FAIR AND AFFLUENT SABBATH OF MY MUSE": rough draft, pencil, unsigned, Notebook 15, pp. 27–30. Allusions are to Wilfrid and Alice Meynell.

A POET'S TESTAMENT: rough draft, pencil, unsigned, Notebook B.C. 14, pp. 36–37. Similarity of sentiment, identity of technique and the fact that the first draft of *From the Night of Forebeing* is in the same notebook, suggest that these lines may have been written as part of that poem. But there is no indication of where the poet intended to insert them.

A QUESTION: final draft, ink, signed. The same title is given a different poem in Thompson's *Collected Poems.* A line from Cowley, quoted by Thompson in connection with *Assumpta Maria,* is equally pertinent here: "Thou needst not make new songs, but say the old."

INDEX OF FIRST LINES